AMERICAN POLITICAL, ECONOMIC, AND SECURITY ISSUES

FINANCIAL INFORMATION SOURCES

SCOPE OF EDUCATION AND MARKETING ACTIVITIES

AMERICAN POLITICAL, ECONOMIC, AND SECURITY ISSUES

Additional books in this series can be found on Nova's website under the Series tab.

Additional e-books in this series can be found on Nova's website under the e-book tab.

AMERICAN POLITICAL, ECONOMIC, AND SECURITY ISSUES

FINANCIAL INFORMATION SOURCES

SCOPE OF EDUCATION AND MARKETING ACTIVITIES

DANA VOGEL
EDITOR

NOVINKA

New York

For permission to use material from this book please contact us:
Telephone 631-231-7269; Fax 631-231-8175
Web Site: http://www.novapublishers.com

Additional color graphics may be available in the e-book version of this book.

Library of Congress Cataloging-in-Publication Data

ISBN: 978-1-63117-040-9

Published by Nova Science Publishers, Inc. † New York

CONTENTS

PREFACE

This book discusses a comparison of spending on financial education and financial marketing, and an overlap of programs that suggest there may be opportunities for consolidation.

Chapter 1 – The Consumer Financial Protection Bureau (the CFPB) looked at the information sources consumers are exposed to when they make financial decisions. Empowering consumers to make the financial decisions that will help them meet their own life goals is a critical part of the mission of the CFPB. To understand the wide range of information sources consumers could be exposed to in making financial decisions, the CFPB commissioned a study of the size and scope of the financial information field.* The results give an overall indication of the relative amounts spent in the U.S. on financial education and on the marketing of certain types of financial products. Though the results should not be treated as precise measures of spending, we hope the study encourages further research and stimulates discussion on the scope and role of financial education.

In the U.S. economy, billions of dollars are spent on financial industry marketing efforts, about 25 times more than is spent on financial education. The study found that approximately *$670 million* is spent annually on providing financial education by federal, state, and local governments, financial institutions, nonprofit organizations, charitable foundations, and others. At the same time, the financial services industry spends approximately *$17 billion* annually marketing consumer financial products and services (not counting marketing of products related to retirement, college loans, and other investments). While the study does not explore the effect of this spending disparity on consumer decisions, it provides a meaningful comparison when we consider consumers' financial educational needs.

Chapter 2 – Financial literacy—the ability to use knowledge and skills to manage financial resources effectively—plays an important role in helping to ensure the financial health and stability of individuals and families. Federal agencies promote financial literacy through activities including print and online materials, broadcast media, individual counseling, and classroom instruction. In response to a mandate requiring GAO to identify duplicative government programs and activities, this report addresses (1) the cost of federal financial literacy activities; (2) the extent of their overlap and fragmentation; (3) the federal government's coordination of these activities; and (4) what is known about their effectiveness. GAO reviewed agency budget documents, strategic plans, performance reports, websites, and other materials, and interviewed representatives of federal agencies and other organizations.

In: Financial Information Sources
Editor: Dana Vogel
ISBN: 978-1-63117-040-9

Chapter 1

NAVIGATING THE MARKET: A COMPARISON OF SPENDING ON FINANCIAL EDUCATION AND FINANCIAL MARKETING*

Consumer Financial Protection Bureau

EXECUTIVE SUMMARY

The Consumer Financial Protection Bureau (the CFPB) looked at the information sources consumers are exposed to when they make financial decisions. Empowering consumers to make the financial decisions that will help them meet their own life goals is a critical part of the mission of the CFPB. To understand the wide range of information sources consumers could be exposed to in making financial decisions, the CFPB commissioned a study of the size and scope of the financial information field.* The results give an overall indication of the relative amounts spent in the U.S. on financial education and on the marketing of certain types of financial products. Though the results should not be treated as precise measures of spending, we hope the study encourages further research and stimulates discussion on the scope and role of financial education.

---

* This is an edited, reformatted and augmented version of the Boston Consulting Group publication, under contract with the Consumer Financial Protection Bureau, dated November 18, 2013.

In the U.S. economy, billions of dollars are spent on financial industry marketing efforts, about 25 times more than is spent on financial education. The study found that approximately *$670 million* is spent annually on providing financial education by federal, state, and local governments, financial institutions, nonprofit organizations, charitable foundations, and others. At the same time, the financial services industry spends approximately *$17 billion* annually marketing consumer financial products and services (not counting marketing of products related to retirement, college loans, and other investments). While the study does not explore the effect of this spending disparity on consumer decisions, it provides a meaningful comparison when we consider consumers' financial educational needs.

As a nation, we spend about two dollars per person per year on financial education. The $670 million in spending translates to a little more than $2 per person per year on financial education in the U.S. (Note that this figure should be treated as a general order of magnitude of spending rather than a precise estimate, as this number is derived from a modeling methodology with specific assumptions detailed below). In comparison, the $17 billion in financial services marketing translates to about $54 per person per year.

1. Background

The Dodd-Frank Wall Street Reform and Consumer Protection Act of 2010 established the Consumer Financial Protection Bureau (the CFPB) to regulate the offering and provision of consumer financial products or services under federal consumer financial laws. The Act also established the Office of Financial Education within the CFPB, which is responsible for developing and implementing initiatives intended to educate and empower consumers to make better informed financial decisions.

The Office of Financial Education works to promote effective and high-quality financial education for American consumers. To do this, it is helpful to understand the size and scope of today's financial information marketplace in order to calibrate financial education efforts in the context of the broad array of financial information consumers receive.

Financial information comes to the U.S. public from many sources, including nonprofit organizations, financial institutions, governmental agencies, and others. Before this study, we had limited data about the scope and scale of the efforts put forth through these sources, especially the total dollar amount spent to reach consumers.

Beyond just the amount of information received, an important consideration from the consumer's perspective is the information's purpose. Some information is intended to educate consumers, and some is intended to drive a purchase decision. To better understand the influences on consumer behavior, we examined and compared these information sources.

2. Scope of the Study

We have investigated the size and scope of financial information provided to consumers in the United States by estimating how much is spent on providing financial information. We divided financial information into two categories: financial education and financial services marketing.

We defined financial education for the purposes of this study as follows:

> ***Financial Education*** *represents a process of lifelong knowledge and skills development required to achieve financial literacy, learn to mitigate financial risks, protect assets and ensure on-going effective management of one's savings, credit, debt, housing and other resources to maximize financial well-being of individuals and society.*

We took a one-year snapshot of spending in the United States on financial education. We included services such as housing counseling, credit counseling, school-based financial education, financial counseling and coaching, and community-based financial education.

We excluded spending related to investments, insurance, retirement assets and planning, and college loans, aid, and planning. We also excluded financial education that is directly paid for by the consumer, such as money spent on fee-based financial planning, fee-based credit counseling, and books on financial topics. And, we excluded fixed costs, such as the salaries of schoolteachers who provide financial education as part of the courses that they teach.

In addition, the study separated out spending that directly supports the provision of financial education to consumers from spending that supports the financial education field. Direct provision of financial education includes costs associated with services that directly serve consumers, such classes and workshops, one-on-one coaching and counseling, informational website and brochures for consumers, and the like. Supporting services include services such as funding to other organizations (including those that directly provide financial education), technical assistance, training, research and evaluation services, conferences, etc., that help financial education service providers do their work. The delineation between these two types of financial education services is not always completely crisp, and in some cases these services cannot be easily separated in practice. For example, it is sometimes not possible to get data that separates the cost of developing a financial education curriculum from the cost of using it with consumers. As such, the estimates documented here are necessarily imprecise, but we think it is a useful analytic framework to distinguish between direct service and supporting services.

In this analysis, we focused primarily on estimating the spending on direct provision of financial education. We do not provide a detailed estimate of the total amount of spending on support services or a total estimate of direct services and support services together, in part due to the difficulty of getting an estimate that accurately separates out funding from other types of supporting services. If funding is not separated out, it will be double-counted in both direct and supporting services, leading to an erroneous estimate.

However, the limited focus in this report on supporting services does not imply that these services are unimportant. Both of these types of activities – the direct provision of financial education to consumers and the funding, technical assistance, training, research and evaluation, conferences, etc., that help financial education service providers do their work – are crucial components of effectively assisting consumers manage their financial lives.

First, the study looked at providers and funders of financial education, including:

- Federal government
- State governments
- Local governments
- School districts
- Nonprofit organizations
- Financial institutions
- Private philanthropies

Because comprehensive data sources on financial education do not currently exist, we estimated the amount each of these sources spent on financial education by using a methodology that included interviews with experts, public data, 990 tax form data, and other sources to create models to estimate spending by sector. (See the Appendix for a full description of the methodology). Because this is an estimate based on a modeling methodology, the findings should be treated as a general order of magnitude of spending rather than as a precise number.

Next, the study estimated the amount spent by the financial services industry on marketing products and services to consumers. The team further analyzed spending by channel (for example, television, radio, and newspapers) and product type (for example, credit cards). As with the financial education estimate, the marketing analysis excluded spending related to investments, insurance, retirement assets and planning, and college loans, aid, and planning.

We found it was relatively straightforward to analyze spending on marketing, since the industry has established standard measurement techniques. We examined awareness advertising and direct marketing. Awareness advertising tends to reach audiences through traditional channels, such as television, radio and newspapers, while direct marketing spend includes such efforts as Internet advertising, direct mail, and other methods aimed at prompting individuals to make an immediate purchase or at generating leads. The total of these two types gives us an estimate of the overall dollar amount spent by financial institutions on promoting consumer financial products.

Note that the spending estimates across all sectors are not drawn from the same calendar year, due to limitations in data sources. For example, the federal government spending data is 2010 data, drawn from a U.S. General Accounting Office report that gathered data from 2010. The nonprofit data is primarily from tax year 2011, as that is the most recent data available from the Internal Revenue Service. The financial services marketing data is primarily 2012 data. Data from other sectors are drawn from a range of several years, in all cases using the most recent data available. Because the data by sector is not all from the same year, caution should be used in comparing the annual spending sources presented below.

3. Findings

3.1. Annual Financial Education Spending

Using the methodology discussed above and further detailed in the appendix, we found that **annual spending on direct provision of financial education in the U.S. totaled approximately $670 million**. This number provides a sense of the order of magnitude of financial education spending in the United States, not a precise measure.

There are many thousands of individual providers of financial education, and there is currently no straightforward way to uncover and aggregate their budgets and spending. Therefore, as part of the study, we developed assumptions and a model to estimate the total spending from the nation's many financial education providers. (See the Appendix for a full description of the methodology). We hope that further investigation and discussion can refine the estimate and provide a deeper understanding of financial education spending.

Spending on financial education comes from multiple sources, as detailed below.

Federal Government

The federal government spends approximately $230 million on financial education; of this total, approximately $130 million is spent on direct provision of financial education. The remaining $100 million is spent on supporting services around financial education, including services such as grants and contracts to other organizations (including those that directly provide financial education), technical assistance, training, and research.

To estimate the federal government's contribution to the overall financial education market in the United States, we relied on a 2012 U.S. General Accounting Office (GAO)[1] report that provided spending estimates for the majority of federal agencies with presence in this area of work. To preserve data consistency and comparability of baseline results, we utilized the 2012 GAO Report spending levels, with two key caveats:

- The 2012 GAO Report relied on FY 2010 data; thus, the numbers reported do not reflect changes in agency spending since then.
- The Report provided estimates based on assessments by federal agency staff, which were not always consistent across different agencies. For examples, agencies took different approaches as to whether staff time, costs of contracts, printing, etc. were included.

In addition to 2012 GAO Report estimates, we added the CFPB contribution to financial education of approximately $26 million based on the FY2013 budget. (As the CFPB was not in existence in 2010, we could not use a 2010 figure to be comparable to the GAO numbers).

We estimated the breakdown of federal spending into direct service and supporting services categories by examining publically available program descriptions and interviews with agency staff.

Our research found that the federal spending on financial education is heavily concentrated on housing-related services, such as housing counseling and foreclosure mitigation. Some of the federal housing-related support included in the estimate is time-limited in nature; for example, the National Foreclosure Mitigation Counseling Program is a time-limited program.

State Government

State governments spend approximately $67 million on financial education. Of this total, approximately $7 million is spent on direct provision of financial education. The remaining $60 million is spent on supporting services around financial education, including services such as funding to other organizations (including those that directly provide financial education), technical assistance, training, and research.

We conducted analysis to identify spending on financial education in all 50 states as well as the District of Columbia. For each state, a database-driven search of recent news reports was supplemented with more detailed research on state budgets and legislative updates. A state-by- state analysis was also completed to understand how each state is allocating its award from the National Mortgage Settlement. In addition, we supplemented this data through interviews with a small group of state and city government officials. Based on interviews and expert input, we considered 90 percent of state spending as supporting services (e.g., grants, training, etc.).

A significant portion of state spending is derived from the National Mortgage Settlement funds that many states have been using for housing-related financial education, including housing counseling and foreclosure mitigation counseling. For the purposes of this study, the funding was assumed to be spread over a five-year period, as interviews and expert input suggested that many states would be spending these funds over this length of time. Thus, one-fifth of states' spending on financial education from this source was considered the annual spending. As these resources represent a one-time source of funding, states' funding of financial education after this five-year investment may be significantly lower.

Municipal and School District Funding

Municipal governments and school districts together spend approximately $46 million on financial education. Of this total,

approximately $31 million is spent on direct provision of financial education. The remaining $19 million is spent on supporting services around financial education, such as funding to other organizations (including those that directly provide financial education), technical assistance, training, and research.

Municipal Government

To assess local government investments in financial education, we conducted interviews with representatives of city governments across the country. Findings from these interviews suggested notable disparities in levels of attention and resources devoted to financial education among cities.

New York City provided an example of a high level of local government support for financial education supported by a stable funding stream through a dedicated levy, raising approximately $2,500,000 per year for the city of 8.2 million inhabitants. However, even at this level of funding, per capita local government expenses for financial education amount to approximately thirty cents per person annually.

Our analysis suggested that New York City level of expenditures represents the upper bound for local government support provided to financial education. If New York's funding level of approximately thirty cents is extrapolated to the United States population of 313 million, total local government funding available across the country could reach as high as $94 million.

To estimate the lower bound of local government resources devoted to financial education, we assumed that every township/town, municipality and county invests $1,000 per year. With 38,917 local government entities across the country, this assumption yielded the nation-wide lower bound local government spending for financial education of $39 million.

Overall, we estimate that local government funding for financial education amounts to $39-94 million per year. We have opted to use the lower boundary for our overall municipal estimate, as our analysis suggests that New York City is an outlier in providing significant spending on financial education because of its dedicated levy, and spending levels across other cities appears to be much lower.

Using this lower boundary, based on expert interviews, we estimated that $31 million of the $39 million was used for direct provision of financial education by local governments.

School Districts

To assess additional funding available for financial education and provided through individual school districts, we conducted a series of interviews with secondary school education professionals representing school systems, academia, city governments and the non-profit community. The interviews aimed to identify a range of funding levels, with the following caveats:

- Teachers' salaries and other personnel expenses are out-of-scope.
- The study does not account for portions of textbooks and other materials that may contain financial education components (e.g., economics textbooks containing financial education concepts).

Thus, we are estimating spending on school-based financial education beyond the important efforts teachers may be making in a classroom setting in many places.

In general, the interviews revealed that only minimal funding, beyond funds spent on teacher salaries or textbooks that include financial education, is available for financial education at the school district level. Interviews also revealed that some financial education in schools is provided or enabled by nonprofit organizations, financial institution staff, or others. As this is not paid for by the school districts, those efforts are not captured in this section but appear in the relevant spending estimates for other sectors.

However, we identified examples of financial education funding at the school district level that supported professional development opportunities around financial education for teachers. Typically this entails covering travel, registration fees, stipends, substitute teacher expenses and other related items to support teachers attending financial education training. Based on what we heard in interviews, we made several assumptions to estimate the amount of these financial education expenses available through school districts:

- The average financial education teacher training costs about $500/teacher.
- The average school district sends 1-3 teachers to these trainings per district/year.
- Thus, the average spending on financial education teacher training amounts to $500-1,500 per district/year. All of this spending is considered to be supporting services.

Based on 2012 Digest of Education Statistics, there are currently 13,588 school districts across the United States. With $500-1,500 invested in financial education teacher training by every district, the total financial education spending by school districts amounts to $7-21 million per year.

Financial Institutions

Financial institutions spend approximately $160 million on financial education. Of this total, approximately $31 million is spent on direct provision of financial education. The remaining $129 million is spent on supporting services around financial education, such as funding to other organizations (including those that directly provide financial education), technical assistance, training, and research.

Financial institutions, typically through their charitable foundations, contribute funding to other organizations that directly provide financial education to consumers. In addition, many financial institutions provide some financial education directly; for example, their staff may participate in community financial education sessions, or they may create financial education materials for consumers. While we did not count the monetary value of in-kind staff time, we did include other costs associated with such efforts, such as tools and materials used by staff in directly providing financial education.

To estimate spending on financial education by financial institutions, we gathered information via interviews with representative firms and supplemented this with data gathered from publicly available sources. We then extrapolated from the spending by representative firms to estimate spending for the broader sector. Specific steps included the following:

- We interviewed banks among the top 15 largest in the U.S. and captured specific information on the expenditures and reach of their financial education initiatives.
- We reviewed press coverage, annual reports, and Corporate Social Responsibility reports for financial education-related initiatives of other financial institutions including banks, audit and advisory firms, and credit card companies.
- Based on these sources, we isolated actual spending on financial education from other contributions such as labor hours and in-kind donations.
- We estimated bank spending on financial education based on the known investments of eight of the top 15 banks using the proportion

of their assets to the total assets in the U.S. banking sector as a basis for extrapolation.

- We estimated financial education spending in the audit/advisory sector based on known commitments from the Big 4 audit/advisory firms using their share of overall U.S. market to extrapolate.
- We captured spending of large credit card companies without having to engage in extrapolation.
- From data gathered in interviews, we estimated that 20% of financial institution spending on financial education is allocated to direct provision of services with the remaining 80% allocated to supporting services.

Private Philanthropies

Philanthropic giving related to financial education exceeds $40 million. All of this funding falls into the category of supporting services for financial education, as opposed to direct provision of services.

Private philanthropic foundations contribute to the cause of financial education over and above resources provided by foundations linked to banks and other financial institutions. To develop an estimate of private foundation giving to financial education, we reviewed 2012 grant-making data for all foundations included in the list of the top 50 largest foundations by size of their asset base. Our review of 2012 data at the level of individual grants and associated descriptions of purpose and intent enabled the team to suggest that the top 50 foundations provide at least $40 million of contributions to financial education. Funding levels are likely higher if private foundations outside of the top 50 are taken into account.

Note that philanthropic giving is considered supportive services; thus, this estimate is not included in the overall direct spending estimate above. The philanthropic funding that supports direct provision of financial education by non-profit organizations is captured in the spending estimates for non-profit organizations (see below).

Non-Profit Organizations

Non-profit organizations spend approximately $550 million on financial education; of this total, approximately $472 million is spent on direct provision of financial education. The remaining $78 million is spent on supporting services around financial education, such as grants, training, research, and other services.

Our analysis of non-profit organizations included the following four categories:

- National/state-level non-profit organizations
- Industry/trade associations and coalitions
- Community-based groups and clubs
- Faith-based organizations

To analyze financial education spending by all four categories of non-profit organizations, we conducted a top-down assessment of financial education spending, created a comprehensive database of non-profit spending data, and classified each non-profit organization along several dimensions. We created assumptions for each classification and applied them to the database in order to estimate total non-profit spending on financial education as well as breakdowns for direct service provision vs. supporting functions. Specific steps included the following:

- We identified an initial list of approximately 30 leading non-profit organizations in the financial education field based on CFPB staff knowledge and contacts.
- We searched a database of Form 990 tax filings using National Taxonomy of Exempt Entities (NTEE) codes applicable to financial education, and also using selected key words. (A list of these NTEE codes and key words can be found in the Appendix). Most of this data is from tax year 2011, although in some cases tax data is from a previous year.
- By combining the list of approximately 30 key organizations with the list generated by the 990 tax filing search, we created a list of approximately 1,200 entities with over $30 billion in combined annual expenses. This list included both large and small non-profit organizations.
- Based on information gathered via interviews with CFPB and other organizations, we reviewed the full list to remove out-of-scope organizations. We also combined organizational families and national associations into a single parent entity.
- We then categorized non-profits on this list into organization types
    - National or State Level
    - Trade Associations & Coalitions
    - Community-Based

    - Faith-Based
- We then classified each organization based on mission focus on financial education and created assumptions for each category to determine the estimated portion of total spending allocated to financial education. (More details on this process are included in the full methodology included as an Appendix).
- We used a modified classification scheme for credit counseling organizations. Since a significant proportion of the budgets of some of these organizations are raised through client fees, and self-funded financial education is out of scope for this study, we removed from the list the credit counseling agencies that receive almost all of their revenue from fees. For credit counseling agencies that also provide other types of free financial education services, we estimated, based on interviews and other data sources, that 15% of their overall budgets were not generated by client fees.
- Combining all of the above data into one model, we estimate that the collective annual spending on financial education by nonprofit organizations is approximately $550 million.
- We reviewed the full list of entities on an organization-by-organization basis to determine distributions of spending by service type (i.e., direct versus supporting services).

Summary of Financial Edcuation Spending

We then summed up the spending on **direct provision** of financial education by all of these sectors – federal government, state government, municipal government, school districts, nonprofits, and financial institutions. (Private philanthropies and school districts were not included as all of their spending is considered supporting services).

Thus, we find that **the total annual spending on direct provision of financial education is approximately $670 million**. Of this total, approximately three-quarters of the total spending comes from private sources, and the remaining one-quarter comes from all public sources combined.

Note that the total spending across all sectors cannot be added to get an accurate total of both direct service and supporting services for financial education. The supporting service component of this analysis includes funding that is given to other organizations, and that spending may then also be captured in the direct service budgets for those organizations, or in the supporting services provided by those organizations. Thus, summing the overall direct provision spending and the support service spending would contain a very significant amount of double counting. Removing double-counting from the supporting services spending category would require significant additional analysis that is beyond the scope of this study.

Looking at annual spending on financial education on a per capita basis, the nation spends just above **two dollars per person per year on financial education** from both public and private sources (based on our $670 million estimate of annual spending and the current U.S. population of approximately 314 million people).[2]

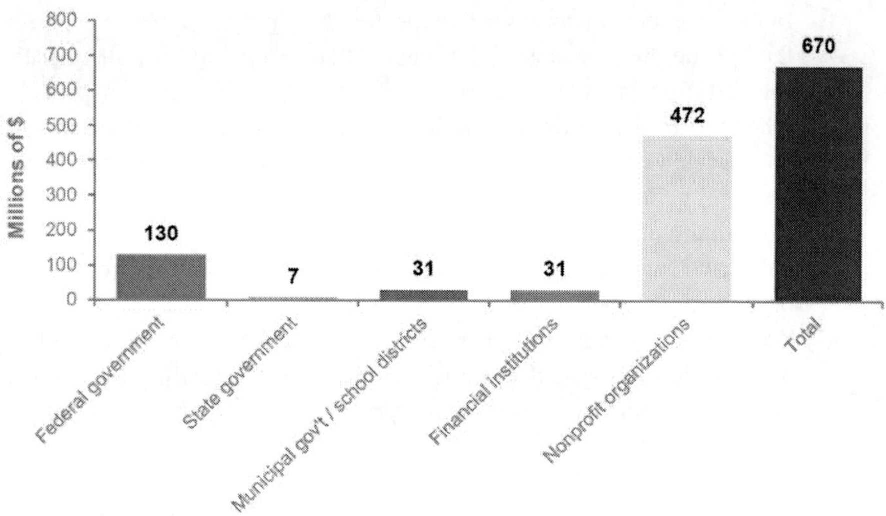

Figure 1. Direct Annual Financial Education Spending by All Sources.

3.2. Financial Services Industry Marketing Spending

We then turned to the spending by financial service providers to market their products. This marketing constitutes another source of information that consumers are exposed to when making financial decisions. We found that **the total amount spent annually by financial institutions and other financial service providers on consumer financial products and services, including both awareness advertising and direct marketing, is approximately $17 billion.**

The marketing spending analysis followed the same scope guidelines used for the financial education spending analysis above (i.e., spending related to investments, insurance, retirement assets and planning, and college loans, aid, and planning were excluded).

We obtained comprehensive data and developed robust assumptions covering the full scope of the analysis for a single year (2012). All channel-specific and product-specific findings pertain to the full calendar year 2012.

Using methods detailed below and in the Appendix, we developed an estimate of the dollar amount spent by the financial services industry on marketing consumer financial products. We further analyzed the marketing spending and delineated spending by channel (e.g., TV, radio, newspapers) and product type (e.g., credit cards).

We segmented the analysis into general awareness advertising spending and direct marketing spending. Awareness advertising tends to reach audiences through traditional channels, such as television, radio and newspapers, while direct marketing includes such channels as Internet display advertising, direct mail and other methods aimed at prompting individuals to make an immediate purchase or generate a lead.

Awareness Advertising Spending

Financial services providers spend approximately $5.5 billion on awareness advertising annually. Based on the methodology detailed below and in the Appendix, we found that the financial service providers spent approximately $5.5 billion on awareness advertising per year (based on a one-year sample). Awareness advertising includes delivering general promotional messages not intended for immediate sales of products, through channels such as television, radio, newspapers, and the like.

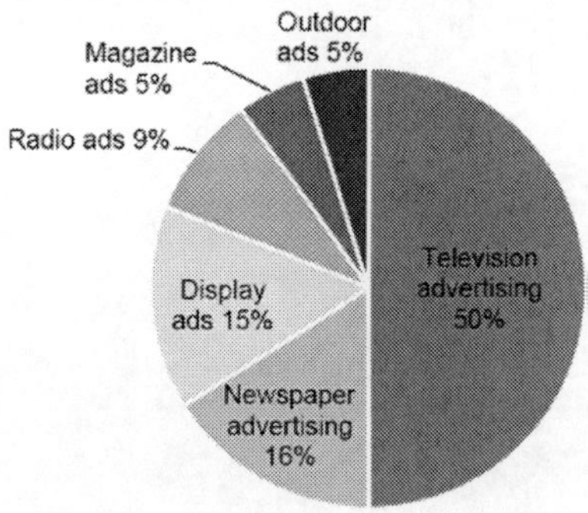

Figure 2. Annual Awareness Adverstising by Media Type.

We found that awareness advertising spending on financial products and services broke down by **media type** in the following way:

- **50%** of the $5.5 billion was spent on **television advertising**
- **16%** was spent on **newspaper advertising**
- **15%** was spent on **display ads**
- **9%** was spent on **radio ads**
- **5%** was spent on **magazine ads**
- **5%** was spent on **outdoor ads** (for example, billboards)

The awareness advertising can also be broken down by **product type**:

- **56%** of approximately $5.5 billion in awareness advertising was spent on **credit- and loan-related products** (including credit cards, mortgages, vehicle loans, and home equity loans)
- **24%** was spent on advertising related to **banking services** (including checking, savings, and general banking promotion)
- **19%** was spent on advertising related to **other services** (including ATM networks, credit counseling, check cashing, and consumer financial promotions)

More than 40% of the approximately $5.5 billion spent on awareness advertising is spent on marketing credit cards. When the marketing of other products such as mortgages and vehicle loans are added, more than half of awareness advertising spending is devoted to credit products, as opposed to other banking and financial services.

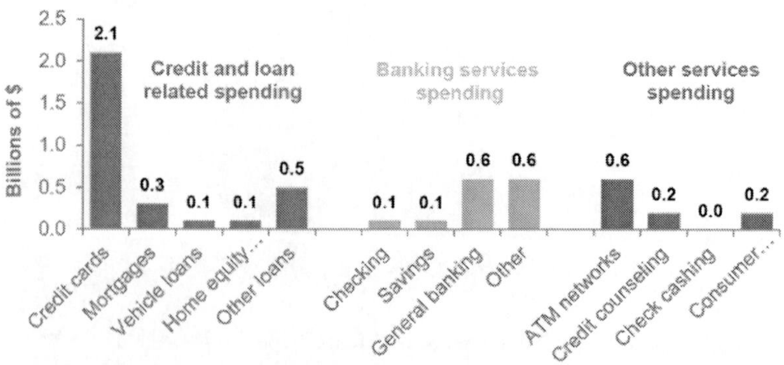

Figure 3. Annual Awareness Adverstising by Product Type.

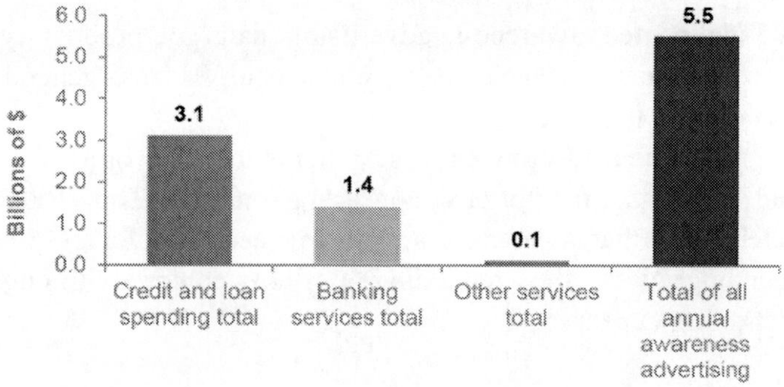

Figure 4. Comparison of Annual Awareness Advertising by Product Category.

To develop the estimates presented above, we took the following steps:

- We obtained granular campaign-specific data for awareness advertising campaigns conducted by financial institutions across the U.S. in 2012.
    - We utilized data aggregated in an advertising spending database populated with individual advertising data points from 24/7 electronic monitoring, newspaper and magazine scans, billboard reporting, etc.
    - The database covers reporting by approximately 6,000 financial institutions and includes all reported ad efforts and campaigns.
    - For purposes of the current study, the team extracted spending details for approximately 35,000 individual ad campaigns conducted in 2012.
- We removed business product spending items (e.g., corporate credit card ads), and spot checked and correlated with AdAge reporting for key financial institutions
- We aggregated individual campaign entries for key general advertising channels:
    - TV
    - Magazines
    - Newspapers
    - Radio
    - Display
    - Outdoor
- We developed full year 2012 total estimates for each channel and a grand total for all awareness advertising.

- We delineated awareness advertising data by product type (e.g., mortgage loans, vehicle loans, home equity loans, general banking services).
- We reviewed marketing expense patterns for 100 Top U.S. advertisers and financial institutions appearing on the Top 100 list and determined that awareness advertising accounts for 30-50% of the spending with the remaining portion captured through direct marketing expenses.

Direct Marketing Spending

Financial service providers spend approximately $12 billion on direct marketing annually. Based on the methodology detailed below and in the Appendix, we found that the financial service providers spent approximately $12 billion on direct advertising per year (based on a one-year sample). Direct marketing includes such channels as Internet display advertising, direct mail and other methods aimed at prompting individuals to make an immediate purchase or generate a lead.

We found that direct marketing spending on financial products and services broke down by **media type** in the following way:

- **44 %** of the approximately $12 billion in direct marketing was spent on **internet display and search**
- **16%** was spent on direct response **television advertising**
- **22%** was spent on **direct mail**
- **5%** was spent on direct response **newspaper ads**
- **3%** was spent on direct response **magazine ads**
- **4%** was spent on **social networking**
- **2%** was spent on direct response **radio ads**
- **2%** was spent on **advertising emails**
- **2%** was spent on other methods

To develop the above estimates of U.S. financial institutions' direct marketing expenses aimed at promoting consumer financial products, we took the following steps:

- We analyzed direct marketing data and reports from Direct Marketing Association, Inc., Kantar, Schonfeld and other sources to identify direct patterns and robust data capture mechanisms.
- We confirmed the level of spending typical for financial institutions.

- We also used direct marketing spending data reported in The Power of Direct Marketing, 2011-2012 Edition.
- We grouped data to capture spending on key direct marketing channels:
    - Direct response components of TV, radio, newspapers and magazines
    - Direct mail
    - Internet display, search, social networking, commercial e-mail
- We applied spending proportions to break out direct marketing spend by channel for each product type (e.g., mortgages, vehicle loans, credit cards, home equity loans).

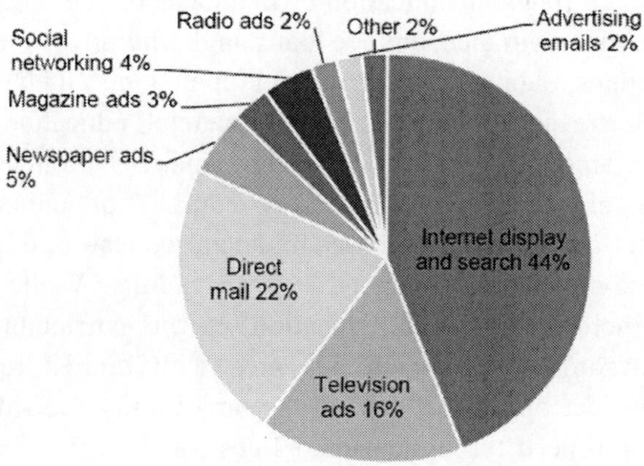

Figure 5. Direct Marketing Spending by Media Type.

Summary of Financial Services Industry Marketing Spending

By combining the assessments (detailed above) of the two marketing spending components – about **$5.5 billion in awareness advertising** and **$12 billion in direct marketing** – we created an estimate of the overall dollar amount spent by financial institutions on promoting consumer financial products. We found that the total amount spent annually by financial institutions and other financial service providers is approximately **$17 billion**.

Looking at this spending on marketing on a per capita basis, **financial services providers spend approximately $54 per person per year on marketing of consumer financial products and services** (based on our $17 billion estimate of annual spending and the current U.S. population of approximately 314 million people).

CONCLUSION

Combined, financial institutions and financial educators provide a vast amount of information to the public. This means that for each decision in their financial lives, consumers are probably relying on varying sources of information, each developed with different purposes. This study found a disparity in spending levels on education and marketing—$670 million annually for financial education compared to $17 billion for financial services marketing. This finding indicates that more than 25 times as much is spent on marketing financial products and services to consumers each year than on providing them with financial education. (Note that these estimates do not include spending on financial education or financial service product marketing related to retirement, insurance, college loans, and other investments).

The challenges facing consumers in managing their finances are significant, and the current spending on financial education is very low compared to the amounts spent on marketing financial products. This raises the importance of providing high-quality sources of unbiased financial information. This includes school-based financial education to prepare youth to be able to navigate their financial lives as adults. While many school districts have included financial education in the curriculum, and many teachers do extraordinary work in this area with limited resources, it is important to consider options to expand the opportunity for kids to build the skills that they will need throughout their lives for financial decision-making early and continuously during the K-12 years.

The significant disparity in the magnitude of resources devoted to financial education as opposed to marketing of financial services also suggests the need for financial education and financial skill building opportunities to be provided to Americans in their homes, workplaces, libraries, and through community organizations where they may receive other types of services.

This study suggests that financial educators should further enhance efforts to identify and promote innovative, scalable methods for providing financial education to consumers. Collectively, we need to make financial education resources as effective and innovative as possible in order to maximize our impact in helping American consumers make good financial decisions for themselves and their families.

APPENDIX A. SUMMARY OF METHODOLOGY

Definition of Financial Education

In developing a definition of financial education for the purposes of this study, we relied on comparative analysis of existing definitions for "financial education", "financial literacy", and "financial capability". In particular, we reviewed definitions utilized by the President's Council on Financial Literacy, Financial Literacy Education Commission, Government Accountability Office, Organization for Economic Cooperation and Development, as well as other reputable entities. Upon review of several options, we agreed on the following language for purposes of the study:

> ***Financial Education*** *represents a process of lifelong knowledge and skills development required to achieve financial literacy, learn to mitigate financial risks, protect assets and ensure ongoing effective management of one's savings, credit, debt, housing and other resources to maximize financial well-being of individuals and society.*

To facilitate execution of the study, the team also agreed on an extensive list of definitions, inclusions and exclusions for financial education providers, service types, consumers and supporting organizations. The full listing of definitions is included at the end of this Appendix.

Purpose and Objectives of the Study

The study focused on helping the Consumer Financial Protection Bureau's (CFPB) Office of Financial Education (OFE) to increase understanding of the scope, scale, and funding of providers of financial education and the marketing dollars spent by providers of consumer financial products in the United States. (The research and analysis described in this report was conducted by the Boston Consulting Group under contract with the CFPB).

Design of the study included three task areas defined to achieve the following key objectives:

- Define, delineate and enumerate the types of financial education providers, services and supporting organizations across the United States

- Develop an estimate of the types, funding models, and funding dollar amounts supporting these providers and services
- Develop an estimate of the dollar amount spent by the financial services industry on marketing consumer financial products

The study relied upon publicly available research, IRS Form 990 filings, studies and reports, as well as more than 40 interviews with federal and state government officials, non-profit organizations, financial institutions, local governments, public schools, and other leading experts in the field.

The scope of the study encompassed:

- U.S. market only
- One-year market snapshot
- Financial education market size estimate by provider, type and service type (topics and selected targets)
- Financial service industry marketing spend for consumer financial products by channel as feasible

We defined the following items to be out-of-scope for the current study:

- Services related to securities trading (e.g., stocks and bonds), insurance, retirement assets and planning, and college loans, aid and planning
- Financial education or consumer financial products demand
- Quality measures, consumer satisfaction metrics
- Sales efforts of financial institutions (e.g., call centers, retail sales efforts)
- Financial education strategy
- International efforts/collaboration
- Allocation of fixed costs (e.g., teachers' salaries), except for portions of salaries and fixed costs included in the GAO 2012 Report on Financial Literacy, where these expenses were included in numbers for federal agencies as available
  - No costs were estimated for general curriculum textbooks that may contain financial education components, chapters or exercises
- Services paid for by consumers (e.g., counseling fees)

Financial Education Market Sizing Methodology

In line with the financial education definition, purpose and scope of the Study, we developed and aligned with CFPB on a detailed typology of financial education providers, service types, consumer types and supporting organizations (please see detailed definitions in this Appendix). Defined categories provided the foundation for the financial education market sizing estimate methodology – analysis of the dollar amounts dedicated to financial education by each provider category overall and by service type (e.g., General Financial Education, Housing, Credit Counseling, and Microfinance).

We started by focusing on the following key financial education provider/supporting organization categories:

- Federal government
- State governments
- Non-profit organizations
- Financial institutions
- School districts
- Local governments
- Private philanthropies

For each category, the team determined whether entities within the category serve as financial education providers, supporting organizations or both. For example, federal government agencies fulfill both provider and supporting organization roles, while private philanthropies exclusively serve as supporting organizations. All categories of entities that provide financial education services exclusively or as a part of their operations underwent further analysis to delineate financial education services by type and determine proportions of funding dedicated to specific consumer types.

Analytic techniques and methodology varied by entity category due to data availability, number of entities in each category and other factors. Below are details of analysis steps, assumptions and sources utilized to assess all key provider and supporting organization categories.

Federal Government

To estimate the federal government's contribution to the overall financial education market in the United States, we relied on a 2012 U.S. General

Accounting Office (GAO) report.[3] The GAO Report provided financial education spending estimates for the majority of federal agencies with presence in this area of work.

To preserve data consistency and comparability of baseline results, we utilized the 2012 GAO Report spending levels, clearly defining two key caveats:

- The 2012 GAO Report relied on FY 2010 data.
- The 2012 GAO Report provided estimates based on staff assessments and portions of staff time, costs of contracts, printing, etc. were included, where available.

In addition to the 2012 GAO Report estimates, the team obtained and added the CFPB's contribution to financial education based on the FY2013 budget for financial education of approximately $26 million.

We also examined, but deemed to be out of scope contributions to financial education spending provided by the following entities:

- U.S. Small Business Administration – financial education spending was fragmented across programs and delivered in partnerships with other government and non-profit entities; it was assumed to be captured in other programs included in the study.
- U.S. Commodity Futures Trading Commission – the primary focus is on investor education and fraud prevention, and thus out of scope for the study.

We estimated the breakdown of federal spending into direct service and supporting services categories by examining publically available program descriptions and interviews with agency staff.

State Government

We conducted a thorough analysis to identify spending on financial education in all 50 states as well as the District of Columbia. For each state, a database-driven search of recent news reports was supplemented with more detailed research on state budgets and legislative updates. A state-by-state analysis was also completed to understand how each state is allocating its award from the National Mortgage Settlement.

To determine state spending on financial education, we did the following:

1. Conducted a review of press database to identify financial education grants, initiatives and programs at the state level.
2. Defined agencies most commonly involved in financial education implementation (e.g., State Treasurers, Banking Departments, and Departments of Education) and conducted detailed state-by-state online review of resources committed to financial education.
3. Reviewed activity related to the National Mortgage Settlement by state and determined states/levels associated with financial education; we assumed 5-year spending horizon to determine annual levels, based on information from interviews with experts.
4. Tested financial education spending levels and assumptions through interviews with representatives of state and city governments.
5. Aggregated state-level spending for non-housing-related and housing/National Mortgage Settlement programs across all states.
6. Based on interviews and expert input, we considered 90 percent of state spending as supporting services (e.g., grants, training, etc.).

The following table contains a selection of 10 state programs with accompanying findings about their financial education spending and a sample of sources. Please note, this selection is representative of the detailed data collected for all 50 states and the District of Columbia.

Table 1.

Program	Findings
Arizona - National Mortgage Settlement	Arizona is spending $2 million to raise public awareness and educate the community about the mortgage foreclosure resources available. Arizona is giving $5 million to HUD-approved nonprofit housing counseling agencies so that these agencies can continue to help homeowners.
California - California Department of Education	The California Department of Education is launching a financial literacy awareness campaign. The goal of this initiative is to provide schools, teachers, students and parents with access to supplemental resources that can help students develop a keen understanding of responsible money management and increase their overall financial literacy. The CA Department of Education is partnering with financial institutions, consumer groups, and other government agencies in this effort.

Table 1. (Continued)

Program	Findings
District of Columbia - National Mortgage Settlement	The AG's office plans to spend all settlement funds on mortgage and foreclosure related counseling, legal assistance or advocacy, mediation and outreach assistance to help current and former homeowners secure the benefits they are eligible to receive under the settlement.
Hawaii - National Mortgage Settlement	Hawaii's AG announced intention to distribute $7,911,883 in funds to organizations that support distressed homeowners by providing educational outreach, housing counseling, foreclosure mediation programs, and legal assistance.
Illinois - Department of Treasury	The Department of Financial and Professional Regulation has a course called "Financial Literacy 101". After searching in the budget, we were not able to locate any breakdown for this particular department. The Budget for year 2013 provides the following information: *Securities Investors Education Fund: Appropriation for 2012 – USD 2,333,500*
Maryland - Department of Education	The State Board of Education has adopted regulations requiring local school systems to offer age-appropriate financial literacy education for grades 3 through 12 starting in September 2011. The bill establishing the statewide school program estimated start-up expenses at $152,866 this fiscal year. The education department is determining specifics of the program. It is working with local school systems to develop programs that fit in with existing state curriculum.
New York - National Mortgage Settlement	$9 million sent to support NY Foreclosure Prevention Services Program. $6 million sent to support housing and community renewal activities statewide through not-for-profit community-based housing organizations. The remainder's use is still not clear, though the state recently committed $60 million from the direct settlement towards housing counseling and legal aid services.
Oregon - National Mortgage Settlement	The Executive Board authorized allocating $3.8 million to the Housing and Community Services Department for housing counseling, legal aid, and outreach programs. Later, the Board authorized an additional $3.8 million to the state Department of Justice to support mediation services.
Rhode Island - National Mortgage Settlement	$8.5 million (total award) from National Mortgage Settlement directed to "Foreclosure Protection Program to prevent or reduce the number of initiated foreclosures" - of this, $375,000 to Housing Network of Rhode Island for "homeowner counseling, homebuyer education and outreach" "Empower RI" program in Office of the General Treasurer - funding unclear

Program	Findings
Wisconsin - Department of Administra-tion	The Executive Budget for 2013-2015 states that financial literacy is to be responsibility of Department of Administration, but does not provide any details on amount allocated for financial literacy programs. We checked the Agency Budget Request for Department of Administration (for years 2013-2015) but did not find any additional information. However, the Agency Budget Request for Department of Finan-cial Institutions (attached) provides the following information: *"Investor education and training fund – Total Expenditures: USD 84,500"* *"Payday loan database and financial literacy – Total Expenditures: USD 900,000"*

Local Government

Similar to financial education funding by school districts, a round of interviews also launched assessment of local government investments in financial education. Interviews with representatives of city governments across the country suggested notable disparities in levels of attention and resources devoted to financial education as illustrated by the sampling of quotes obtained via individual interviews:

> ***"Little happening at the city level. A fair amount integrated in city services by non-profit and other partnerships."***
>
> — Director of regional financial education, non-profit organization

> ***"Cities tend to develop relationships with funders and sometimes identify small pools of money to match."***
>
> —Program leader at a city-focused coalition

> ***"New York's Office for Financial Empowerment is funded by a public levy ... of $2.5M a year."***
>
> —NYC city government representative

> ***"Office of the City Treasurer plans to raise $120,000 (same as last year)."***
>
> —Office of the City Treasurer in a major metro area

"City Treasurers across the country do their own things, but are primarily active in major metro areas and locations hard hit by the recent crisis."

—Programs manager at a national network organization

New York City provided an example of high level of local government support for financial education supported by a stable funding stream through a dedicated levy (raising approximately $2.5 million per year for the metro area of 8.2 million inhabitants). However, even at this level of funding per capita local government expenses for financial education amount to thirty cents.

The team suggested that New York City's level of expenditures represents the upper bound for local government support provided to financial education. If New York's funding level of thirty cents is extrapolated to the United States population of 313 million, total local government funding available across the country may reach $94 million.

To estimate the lower bound of local government resources devoted to financial education, the team assumed that every township/town, municipality and county invests $1,000 per year. With 38,917 local government entities across the country, this assumption yielded the nation- wide lower bound local government spending for financial education of approximately $39 million.

Overall, we estimates that local government funding for financial education amounts to $39-94 million per year.

School Districts

To assess additional funding available for financial education and provided through individual school districts, we conducted a series of interviews with secondary education professionals representing school systems, academia, city governments and the non-profit community. The interviews aimed to identify a range of funding levels, accounting for the following caveats defined in the scope of the Study:

- Teachers' salaries and other personnel expenses are out-of-scope.
- The Study does not account for portions of textbooks and other materials that may contain financial education components (e.g., economics textbooks containing financial education concepts).

Across the board, the team established that minimal additional funding is available for financial education at the school district level as illustrated by the following examples of statements obtained through interviews:

> ***"For school districts to kick in any money is quite rare."***
>
> —CEO of a national youth-focused non-profit organization

> ***"School budgets are shrinking and schools are struggling to maintain financial education programs."***
>
> —CEO of a national financial education coalition

> ***"Stock Market Game charges fees that get covered through private donations. Local credit unions provide 1-10K grants."***
>
> —former state Director in the Office of Financial Education

> ***"Minimal additional funding is expected from schools to roll out financial literacy guide."***
>
> —City administration in a major metro area

> ***"Very limited school district resources available across the country. Mandates are basically unfunded."***
>
> —Academic researcher and curriculum development expert

However, we identified examples of financial education funding at the school district level primarily directed at professional education opportunities for financial education teachers. Typical expense categories included travel, registration fees, stipends, substitute teacher expenses and other related items. Based on interview insights the team established key assumptions to estimate the amount of additional financial education -related funds available through school districts:

- Average financial education professional development training cost of $500
- Average teacher training commitment of 1-3 teachers per district/year
- Corresponding training budgets amounting to $500-1,500 per district/year

Based on 2012 Digest of Education Statistics, there are currently 13,588 school districts across the United States. With $500-1,500 invested in financial education by every district, additional financial education spending amounts to $7-21 million per year.

Financial Institutions

Based on the definition of financial institutions agreed upon in the study typology, a varied but rigorous approach was used to estimate spending on financial education by financial institutions. Information gathered via interviews with representative firms was supplemented with data gathered from publicly available sources. Once a fact base was established for a suitable number of entities, extrapolations were performed to estimate spending for the broader sector.

To determine financial institution spending on financial education, we did the following:

1. Interviewed banks among the top 15 largest in the U.S. and captured specific information on the expenditures and reach of their financial education initiatives.
2. Reviewed press coverage, annual reports, and Corporate Social Responsibility reports for financial education-related initiatives of other financial institutions including banks, audit and advisory firms, and credit card companies.
3. Isolated actual spending on financial education from other contributions such as labor hours and in-kind donations.
4. Estimated bank spending on financial education based on the known investments of eight of the top 15 banks using the proportion of their assets to the total assets in the U.S. banking sector as a basis for extrapolation.
5. Estimated financial education spending in the audit/advisory sector based on known commitments from the Big 4 audit/advisory firms using their share of overall U.S. market to extrapolate.
6. Captured spending of key credit card companies without extrapolation.
7. From data gathered in interviews, estimated that 20% of financial institution spending on financial education is allocated to direct provision of service with the remaining 80% allocated to support.
8. Based on known financial education initiatives, allocated financial institution spending across service offerings and consumer segments.

Private Philanthropies

Private philanthropic foundations contribute to the cause of financial education over and above resources provided by foundations linked to banks and other financial institutions. To develop an estimate of private foundation giving to financial education, we reviewed 2012 grant-making data for all foundations included in the list of top 50 largest foundations by size of their asset base. Data for 2012 reviewed at the level of individual grants and associated descriptions of purpose and intent enabled us to suggest that top 50 foundations provide at least $40 million of contributions to financial education. Funding levels are likely higher if private foundations outside of the top 50 are taken into account.

Non-Profit Organizations

A component of the study focusing on non-profit organizations included analysis of four non- profit categories:

- National/state-level non-profit organizations
- Industry/trade associations and coalitions
- Community-based groups and clubs
- Faith-based organizations

To analyze financial education spending by all four categories of non-profit organizations, we conducted a top-down assessment of financial education spending, created a comprehensive database of non-profit spending data, and classified each non-profit organization along several dimensions. Assumptions were created for each classification and applied to the database in order to estimate total non-profit spending on financial education as well as breakdowns for service provision vs. support, consumer segments, and service offerings.

To determine non-profit spending on financial education, we did the following:

1. Identified initial list of approximately 30 leading non-profit organizations in the financial education field.
2. Determined NTEE (National Taxonomy of Exempt Entities) codes applicable to financial education:

- P51: Financial Counseling, Money Management
- S02: Management & Tech.
- S31: Urban, Community
- S43: Mgmt. Services for Small Business/Entrepreneurs
- B03: Prof. Societies & Associates
- B30: Vocational Technical
- B60: Audit, Continuing Education
- B90: Educational Services
- O53: Business, Youth Development
- V22: Economics

3. Searched database of Form 990 tax filings using NTEE codes listed above along with selected key words (note that most of this data is from tax year 2011, although in some cases tax data is from a previous year):
   - Financial literacy
   - Financial education
   - Financial counseling
   - Money management
   - Microfinance
   - Small business management
   - Housing counseling
   - Housing education
4. Generated initial list of approximately 1,200 entities with over $30 billion in combined annual expenses. Augmented list with organizations identified by CFPB, interviewees, and research. List included both large and small non-profit organizations.
5. Based on information gathered via interviews with CFPB and other organizations, reviewed the full list to remove out-of-scope organizations and true-up expenses for in-scope organizations.
6. Combined organizational families and national associations into a single parent entity.
7. Categorized non-profits into organization types
   - National or State Level
   - Trade Associations & Coalitions
   - Community-Based
   - Faith-Based
   - Credit Counselors

8. Classified each organization based on mission focus on financial education and created assumptions for each category to determine the estimated portion of total spending allocated to financial education
9. Leveraged research on individual organizations, interviews and expert input to develop assumptions on financial education spending provider/supporting services split.

Overall Financial Education Market Sizing Estimate

In order to estimate the total market size for spending on financial education, the subtotals for each financial education provider (described above) were aggregated along several dimensions.

Table 2. Portion of Total Expenses Allocated to Financial Education

Code	Description	Value
High	Organizations that devote significant spending to financial education	90%
Med	Organizations with meaningful spending on financial education	30%
CC	Credit counselors that invest in financial education	15%
Low	Organizations with low spending on financial education	5%
Other	Other non-profit organizations	2.8%
Min	Organizations with minimal spending on financial education	1%
Natl	Broad-based, national organizations	0.5%

The primary view of spending on financial education is broken down into two components: spending on the provision of services and spending on support. Because some spending on support represents re-grants from one organization to another, it is not possible to sum the provider and support totals, as this will include some double-counting of funds passed through to service providers. Therefore, these two numbers must be considered independently. We include only the sum for the direct provision of financial education here.

Since data for the federal government and state governments are well known, these subtotals were expressed without ranges. Subtotals for local governments and school districts were expressed with sizable ranges as a result of the methodology used to derive the estimates. For non-profit organizations and financial institutions, it was assumed that the initial estimates represented the lower end of a range of possible spending. Therefore, an upper bound was estimated to be 10% above the lower bound, with some rounding to express ranges in whole numbers.

One final view was presented to illustrate sources and uses of funds. Sources of funds include total spending (the sum of money allocated to provision of service and money allocated to support) for each financial education provider except non-profit organizations. The un- quantified remainder is assumed to be money raised through other giving, such as individual philanthropic contributions. Uses of funds include all money allocated to the provision of services by each financial education provider along with an un-quantified sum attributed to evaluation, research, assessment, and other types of support, except re-granting.

Cross-Checks

Throughout the study, a number of cross-checks were employed to re-validate the reasonable nature of presented estimates. A sampling of key cross-check mechanisms included:

Bottom-up estimates of non-profit spending

Interviews were conducted with key financial education representatives in New York City and Baltimore. Based on these interviews, a list of non-profits was developed and systematized for each city. Spending data was gathered from the Forms 990, and the organizations were categorized according to the study typology. Total spending for each city was then calculated and divided by the city's population in order to estimate financial education spending per capita. These values formed the basis for extrapolation to the overall population of the United States, and the resulting values were used to validate that the top-down estimate of non-profit spending was sound.

Verifying bank donations to major non-profits

After estimating financial education spending by financial institutions based on the methodology described above, the resulting data was cross checked against known donations to major non-profit organizations involved in financial education. It was determined that the financial institution estimates were sufficiently large to cover both known donations and other programs mentioned in annual financial and Corporate Social Responsibility reports.

Financial Services Industry Marketing Spending Methodology

Relying on leading industry methods, we developed an estimate of the dollar amount spent by the financial services industry on marketing consumer financial products. We further analyzed the marketing spending and delineated spending by channel (e.g., TV, radio, newspapers) and product type (e.g., credit cards). We determined that analysis by consumer segment would not be practical and would not add value in the current context.

Marketing spending analysis followed scope guidelines established for the overall project. For example, retirement planning, insurance, college savings products, and other investments were excluded.

We obtained comprehensive data and developed robust assumptions covering the full scope of the analysis for a single year (2012) and all channel-specific and product-specific findings pertain to the full calendar year 2012.

Following marketing industry established analysis techniques, we segmented the analysis into general awareness advertising ("above the line") measured spending and direct marketing ("below the line") spending. Awareness advertising tends to reach audiences through traditional channels, such as television, radio and newspapers, while direct marketing spending includes such channels as internet display advertising, direct mail and others aimed at prompting individuals to make an immediate purchase or generate a lead.

Awareness Advertising Spending Estimate

We commenced analysis by developing a detailed estimate of the measurable awareness advertising expenditures. In particular, the team took the following steps:

1. Obtained granular campaign-specific data for awareness advertising campaigns conducted by financial institutions across the United State in 2012
    - Utilized inputs aggregated in an advertising spending database populated with individual advertising data points from 24/7 electronic monitoring, newspaper and magazine scans, billboard reporting, etc.
    - The database covers reporting by approximately 6,000 financial institutions and includes all reported ad efforts and campaigns.

- For the purposes of the current study, the team extracted spending details for approximately 35,000 individual ad campaigns conducted in 2012.
- Below is an example of data points that were included in the analysis for each campaign.

Field Name	Value
Included in analysis	Yes/no
Time period	2012
Category	Example: B121 Banking (Consumer)
Sub-category	Example: B121.1 Consumer Banking – Checking
Product	Names of individual products and campaigns were sanitized for purposes of the current Study
Television: Network TV, Spot TV, SLN TV, Cable TV, Syndication	Spending for each category in thousands $US
Magazines: General magazines, Sunday magazines, Hispanic magazines, local magazines	Spending for each category in thousands $US
Newspapers: National newspapers, other newspapers, Hispanic newspapers	Spending for each category in thousands $US
Radio: Network radio, National spot radio, local radio	Spending for each category in thousands $US
Display	Spending for each category in thousands $US
Outdoor	Spending for each category in thousands $US

2. Removed business product spending items (e.g., corporate credit card ads); spot checked and correlated with AdAge reporting for key financial institutions.
3. Aggregated individual campaign entries for key general advertising channels:
    - TV, Magazines, Newspapers, Radio, Display, Outdoor
4. Developed full-year 2012 total estimates for each channel and a grand total for all general advertising.
5. Delineated awareness advertising data by product type (e.g., mortgage loans, vehicle loans, home equity loans, general banking services).
6. Reviewed marketing expense patterns for 100 top U.S. advertisers and financial institutions appearing on the top 100 list and determined that awareness advertising accounts for 30- 50% of the spending, with the remaining portion captured through direct marketing expenses.

Direct Marketing Spending Estimate

To estimate direct marketing expenses of U.S. financial institutions aimed at promoting consumer financial products, we:

1. Analyzed direct marketing data and reports from Direct Marketing Association, Inc., Kantar, Schonfeld and other sources to identify direct marketing patterns and most robust data capture mechanisms.
2. Confirmed level of direct marketing spending typical for financial institutions.
3. Decided to use direct marketing spending results reported in The Power of Direct Marketing, 2011-2012 Edition.
4. Grouped data to capture spending on key direct marketing channels:
   - Direct response components of TV, radio, newspapers and magazines
   - Direct mail
   - Internet display, search, social networking, commercial e-mail
5. Applied awareness spending proportions to break out direct marketing spending by channel for each product type (e.g., mortgages, vehicle loans, credit cards, home equity loans).

Total Financial Services Industry Marketing Spending Estimate

By combining assessments of the two marketing spending components – awareness advertising and direct marketing – we developed an estimate of the overall dollar amount financial institutions spent on promoting consumer financial products. The following channels contain both awareness advertising and direct marketing spending elements: television, magazines, newspapers, radio. Display and outdoor channels utilize only awareness advertising resources. Exclusively direct marketing channels include social networking, Internet display, search and other Internet-related advertising options, as well as commercial e-mail, direct mail and others (e.g., insert media).

Typology and Defintions

Through a series of workshops, we reviewed, refined and agreed on typology categories for providers and supporting organizations to guide execution of the study. We further agreed on definitions, inclusions and exclusions for each typology category (please see details below). Note: in the course of analysis execution, some provider categories (e.g., Certified Financial Planners, or CFPs) were de-prioritized based on initial data analysis and limited scope of financial contributions to financial education market.

Provider Definitions

Table 3. Publicly-Funded

Provider type	Definition	Included in category	Excluded from category
Federal government	Includes all federal agencies offering financial education to consumers	Agencies of the Federal government administering programs in scope of the current project (e.g., as defined in GAO 2012 Report+ CFPB + FEMA)	Agencies and programs focusing on securities trading, college aid, retirement savings and planning
State governments	Includes all state agencies offering financial education to consumers	Agencies of state governments administering programs in scope of the current project	Agencies and programs focusing on securities trading, college aid, retirement savings and planning
School districts	K-12 schools offering financial education as part of elementary, middle and high school curricula or outside the classroom	Public school systems providing financial education programs. Sizing based on funding beyond that provided by state/federal gov'ts and non-profits	Sizing excludes funding from supplemental sources (e.g., federal/state gov'ts or non-profits) Private schools
Local governments	Administrative bodies for specific local areas, e.g., towns or counties with agencies delivering financial education	Agencies of local governments delivering financial education services. Sizing based on funds beyond state/federal/non- profit funding	Agencies of local governments acting solely as pass through mechanisms for state, federal, or non-profit financial education funding or programs (will be captured at state/federal level)

Table 4. Privately-Funded

Provider type	Definition	Included in category	Excluded from category
National/ state-level non-profit organizations	Corporations or associations conducting operations with no profit motive in multiple states and providing financial education services as their primary or sole mission or a substantial part thereof	• Corporations, associations and philanthropic foundations (private and corporate) registered as 501(c)-type entities and stating as mission /core initiatives such areas as financial literacy, money management, financial education, microfinance, credit and debt counseling, housing counseling, budgeting and personal finance • Includes national non- profits with broader missions (e.g., United Way, YMCA)	• Entities not registered as 501(c)-type for tax purposes • Entities not explicitly defining financial education or areas in scope for this project as part of their mandate/ mission/ initiatives • Branches and subsidiaries of nation- wide non-profit organizations (funding captured in consolidated financials)
Industry/ trade associations and coalitions	Organizations founded and funded by for- /non-profit entities and stating financial education initiatives implementation as part of their mandates	501(c)-type entities: Established by financial industry professionals and delivering financial education services Set up by non-profit organizations to coordinate financial education activities Acting as mixed coalitions including gov't, for- and non-profit entities	• Coalitions and industry groupings not registered for tax purposes • Financial industry associations delivering no explicit or regular financial education activities

Provider type	Definition	Included in category	Excluded from category
Community groups and clubs	Community /social entities created and registered to organize like-minded individuals locally or remotely for purposes related to dissemination of financial literacy- related knowledge and skills	Groups registered as 501(c)-type entities stating financial education, financial literacy or money mgmt. as part of mission or core activities	• Groups not registered for tax purposes and not acting as "entities" • Groups not declaring engagement with financial education/ literacy
Faith-based organizations	Organizations established by religious congregations or advancing religious beliefs and offering financial education programming as part of their initiatives	Groups registered as 501(c)-type entities stating financial education, financial literacy or money mgmt. as part of mission or core activities	Groups not registered for tax purposes and not acting as "entities" Groups not declaring systematic engagement with financial education /literacy
Financial institutions	For-profit institutions engaged in delivering consumer financial services that provide financial education	Entities across financial services sector with defined financial education initiatives or programs that are distinct (e.g., separate on-line portal) from regular financial product offerings and information	Financial institution marketing efforts (any resources directly linked to or referencing specific products, or displayed in conjunction with specific products)

Provider type	Definition	Included in category	Excluded from category
Certified financial Planners (CFPs)	Individuals completing CFP Board of Standards initial and on-going certification requirements for the purpose of delivering financial advice to consumers	• Presentations and participation in conferences/ Seminars to address broad sets of planning options without explicit promotion of specific options/strategies • Online resources aimed at promoting general best practices and informing of planning options	• Individualized coaching or • counseling services • On-going professional activities and advisory transactions executed by CFPs • Marketing and sales efforts promoting CFP services or specific products • Materials and publications promoting specific products or financial strategies
Community and 4-year colleges	Vocational, community and 4- year higher education institutions providing financial education	Training and information sessions, materials and resources on personal finance delivered within curriculum and outside of the classroom (e.g., orientation)	• Regular coursework requirements covering concepts related to finance and economics that do not cover personal finance • College financial assistance and aid

Table 5. Service Types

Service type	Definition	Included in category	Excluded from category
General personal financial literacy			
Personal finance and money management	Courses, seminars, and workshops offered to a group covering individual or family financial management (e.g., obtaining, planning, and saving monetary resources)	Activities related to savings, earning, spending credit cards, and and consumer loans	• Retirement planning • Tax management • Insurance Social Security • Benefits • Securities trading

Table 5. (Continued)

Service type	Definition	Included in category	Excluded from category
General financial counseling/ coaching	Advisory services offered to a specific individual or a family based on his/her unique financial situation	Financial education activities and resources focused on budgeting and balancing revenue/ expenses	• Retirement planning • Tax management • Insurance • Social Security benefits • Securities trading
Home ownership			
Mortgages	Financial education services related to loans secured by collateral of specified real estate property	• Financial education activities and materials covering loans for primary residences • Pre-purchase counseling • Post-purchase counseling	• Information on loans for investment properties, summer and second homes • Materials and publications on reverse mortgages
Housing/ foreclosure counseling	Group housing counseling sessions; customized actionable advice on how to avoid foreclosure or what to do if foreclosure is imminent	• Financial education addressing homeowners in default or concerned about their ability to maintain payments • Pre-bankruptcy counseling	Reverse mortgage counseling
Credit and debt management			
Credit reports and scores literacy	Financial education services related to reading, analyzing, communicating and managing reporting information and scores	Workshops and training materials focused on credit scores management, data contained in credit reports, access to information, risks, and impacts of credit scores	• Marketing and sales activities by credit reporting agencies or their representatives • Fee-based access to reports and scores

Service type	Definition	Included in category	Excluded from category
Credit and debt counseling	Customized services offered to explore debt repayment outside of bankruptcy	Financial education programs offered free of charge to consumers with distressed credit ratings	• Fee-based debt restructuring services • On-going financial institution operations resulting in debt restructuring or refinancing
Microfinance			
Individual/ small business financial education	Financial education aimed at individuals interested in launching or currently operating micro-businesses/sole proprietorships	Financial education opportunities focused on separating business and personal finances, budgeting and debt management	• In-depth financial or operations management training courses • College-level Business Administration programs and curricula

Table 6. Supporting Organizations

Supporting organization type	Definition	Included in category	Excluded from category
Federal government	Includes federal agencies offering financial support and technical assistance to entities providing financial education	• Federal financial education grants programs • Financial education - related research and evaluation projects	• Direct financial education service delivery activities • Program components focusing on securities trading, college aid, retirement savings and planning
Financial institutions	Technical support and funding directed to financial education providers from private and public institutions collecting funds from general public or other entities for the purpose of investing in financial assets	Sponsorships and grants Printed materials and online resources and toolkits	• Volunteer time • Seminars, workshops, conferences for financial education consumers (captured in provider category)

Table 6. (Continued)

Supporting organization type	Definition	Included in category	Excluded from category
Private philan-thropies	Private or corporate foundations conducting operations with no profit motive and supplying funds and resources to financial education providers	Sponsorships and grants Printed materials and online resources and toolkits	• Volunteer time • Seminars, workshops, conferences for financial education consumers (captured in provider category)
Industry/ trade associations and coalitions	Organizations founded and funded by for-/non-profit entities and implementing programs in support of financial education providers	Sponsorships and grants Printed materials and online resources and toolkits	• Volunteer time • Seminars, workshops, conferences for financial education consumers (captured in provider category)
National / state-level non-profit organizations	Corporations or associations conducting operations with no profit motive in multiple states and supporting provision of financial education services as their primary mission or a substantial part thereof	Corporations and associations registered as 501(c)-type enti-ties and stating as mission/core initiatives such areas as financial literacy, money management, financial education, microfinance, credit and debt counseling, housing counseling, budgeting and personal finance Includes national non-profits with broad missions (e.g., United Way, YMCA)	• Entities not registered as501(c)-type for tax purposes • Entities not explicitly defining financial education or areas in scope for this project as part of their mandate/mission /initiatives • Branches and subsidiaries of nation-wide non-profit organizations (funding captured in consolidated financials)

Supporting organization type	Definition	Included in category	Excluded from category
Evaluation firms	For-profit providers of information and research services	Grants, sponsor ships and materials delivered to financial education providers free of charge as part of partnership efforts	Paid research products, datasets, studies and recommendations
University-based researchers	University-based (typically non-profit) providers of information and research services	Research products, information and other support provided free of charge as part of partnerships with financial education providers	• Academic research • University/college-level academic curricula and associated materials
Consumer protection groups	Non-profit entities advancing consumer rights, accuracy of information about products and services, and fair competition	Consumer organizations Self-regulating business organizations, e.g., Better Business Bureaus	Government entities

End Notes

[1] GAO, *Report to Congressional Committees on Financial Literacy – Overlap of Programs Suggests There May Be Opportunities for Consolidation*. GAO-12-588 (Washingt0n, DC: Jul. 23, 2012). Note that in its April 2013 report on duplication of federal programs, GAO did not include financial literacy. The report noted that its overall assessment of the two financial literacy areas is that they have been "addressed, meaning all actions needed in that area were addressed." GAO, *2013 Annual Report: Actions Needed to Reduce Fragmentation, Overlap, and Duplication and Achieve Other Financial Benefits*. GAO-13-279SP (Washington, DC: April 2013).

[2] We augmented the estimates with a detailed study of the financial education infrastructure in two cities, Baltimore and New York City. We selected these cities as they represent examples of cities that have strong financial education providers and services. Looking at the budgets of the major providers of financial education (funded by a combination of all the sectors listed above, including funds from multiple levels of government, financial institutions, etc.), we found that spending on financial education in these cities was between $1 and $2.40 per person per year. The additional detail from the city level provides

validation of the national total, as the order of magnitude of financial education spending at the city level ($1 to $2.40) is in the same range as the national estimate of financial education spending (just above $2).

[3] GAO, *Report to Congressional Committees on Financial Literacy – Overlap of Programs Suggests There May Be Opportunities for Consolidation*. GAO-12-588 (Washingt0n, DC: Jul. 23, 2012). Note that in its April 2013 report on duplication of federal programs, GAO did not include financial literacy. The report noted that its overall assessment of the two financial literacy areas is that they have been "addressed, meaning all actions needed in that area were addressed." GAO, *2013 Annual Report: Actions Needed to Reduce Fragmentation, Overlap, and Duplication and Achieve Other Financial Benefits*. GAO-13-279SP (Washington, DC: April 2013).

In: Financial Information Sources
Editor: Dana Vogel
ISBN: 978-1-63117-040-9

Chapter 2

FINANCIAL LITERACY: OVERLAP OF PROGRAMS SUGGESTS THERE MAY BE OPPORTUNITIES FOR CONSOLIDATION*

United States Government Accountability Office

WHY GAO DID THIS STUDY

Financial literacy—the ability to use knowledge and skills to manage financial resources effectively—plays an important role in helping to ensure the financial health and stability of individuals and families. Federal agencies promote financial literacy through activities including print and online materials, broadcast media, individual counseling, and classroom instruction. In response to a mandate requiring GAO to identify duplicative government programs and activities, this report addresses (1) the cost of federal financial literacy activities; (2) the extent of their overlap and fragmentation; (3) the federal government's coordination of these activities; and (4) what is known about their effectiveness. GAO reviewed agency budget documents, strategic plans, performance reports, websites, and other materials, and interviewed representatives of federal agencies and other organizations.

---

* This is an edited, reformatted and augmented version of the Highlights of GAO-12-588, a report to congressional committees, dated July, 2012.

WHAT GAO RECOMMENDS

GAO recommends that CFPB clearly delineate with other agencies respective roles and responsibilities, and that the Financial Literacy and Education Commission identify options for consolidating federal financial literacy efforts and address the allocation of federal resources in its national strategy. CFPB neither agreed nor disagreed with these recommendations and the Department of the Treasury agreed with the recommendations directed to the commission.

WHAT GAO FOUND

The federal government spent about $68 million on 15 of the 16 financial literacy programs that were comprehensive in scope or scale in fiscal year 2010; cost data were not available for the Consumer Financial Protection Bureau (CFPB), which was created that year. In addition, about $137 million in federal funding in four other major programs was directed to housing counseling, which can include elements of financial education. Since fiscal year 2010, at least four of these programs have been defunded and CFPB has received resources to fund its financial literacy activities.

Federal financial literacy and housing counseling activities are spread across multiple agencies and programs. GAO has not identified duplication—programs providing the same activities and services to the same beneficiaries—but has found overlap—multiple programs with similar goals and activities—in areas such as housing counseling and the financial education of youth. Further, CFPB was charged with some financial education duties that overlap with those of other federal agencies, making it essential that their respective roles and responsibilities be clearly delineated to ensure efficient use of resources. Moreover, CFPB's creation may signal an opportunity for consolidating some federal financial literacy efforts, which would be consistent with federal goals of reorganizing and consolidating federal agencies to reduce the number of overlapping government programs.

Federal agencies have made progress in recent years in coordinating their financial literacy activities and collaborating with nonfederal entities, in large part due to the efforts of the federal multiagency Financial Literacy and Education Commission. The commission's 2011 national strategy includes some useful elements—such as plans to coordinate interagency communication, improve strategic partnerships, and promote evaluation. However, it does not recommend or provide guidance on the appropriate allocation of federal resources among programs and agencies, which GAO has found to be desirable in a national strategy. While the commission's governance structure presents challenges in addressing resource issues, without a clear discussion of resource needs and where resources should be targeted, policymakers lack information to help direct the strategy's implementation and help ensure efficient use of funds.

The wide range of federal financial literacy activities and evaluation methods makes it difficult to systematically assess overall effectiveness or compare results across programs. Among the federal financial literacy programs that we reviewed, most included some evaluation component. Some measured the effect on participant behavior and others assessed changes in participant knowledge or tracked output measures, such as the number of consumers reached. Rigorous evaluation measuring behavior change is costly and methodologically challenging and may not be practical for all types of activities. However, CFPB and other federal entities have new efforts under way that seek to determine the most effective approaches and programs, which GAO believes to be positive steps toward helping ensure the best and most efficient use of federal financial literacy resources.

ABBREVIATIONS

CFPB	Consumer Financial Protection Bureau
DOD	Department of Defense
Dodd-Frank Act	Dodd-Frank Wall Street Reform and Consumer Protection Act
FDIC	Federal Deposit Insurance Corporation
FTC	Federal Trade Commission
HUD	Department of Housing and Urban Development
SEC	Securities and Exchange Commission
Treasury	Department of the Treasury

July 23, 2012

The Honorable Tim Johnson
Chairman
The Honorable Richard C. Shelby

Ranking Member
Committee on Banking, Housing, and Urban Affairs
United States Senate

The Honorable Spencer Bachus
Chairman
The Honorable Barney Frank
Ranking Member
Committee on Financial Services
House of Representatives

Financial literacy plays an important role in helping to ensure the financial health and stability of individuals and families, and economic and demographic changes in recent years have further highlighted the need to empower all Americans to make informed financial decisions. The federal government has played a key role in addressing financial literacy, and this role has evolved in recent years, particularly with the creation of the Financial Literacy and Education Commission in 2003 and the Bureau of Consumer Financial Protection, commonly referred to as the Consumer Financial Protection Bureau (CFPB), in 2010. At the same time, however, increasing fiscal constraints at government agencies, particularly with regard to discretionary spending, may limit the resources available for financial literacy efforts, underscoring the need for the most efficient use of these resources.

We have issued a series of reports on potential duplication, overlap, and fragmentation among federal programs, which have included information about financial literacy programs.[1] This report expands on these themes and addresses (1) what is known about the cost of federal financial literacy activities; (2) the extent and consequences of overlap and fragmentation among federal financial literacy activities; (3) what the federal government is doing to coordinate its financial literacy activities; and (4) what is known about the effectiveness of federal financial literacy activities.

To address the first objective, we collected cost information from congressional appropriations, agency budget justifications, and other sources as available. Where costs related to financial literacy were not discrete or clearly apparent from these documents, we worked with agency staff to develop cost estimates. To address the other objectives, we reviewed and analyzed relevant reports and surveys and federal agency strategic plans, performance and accountability reports, websites, budget justifications, performance data, and evaluations related to federal financial literacy efforts.

We also interviewed staff of 17 federal agencies that we had identified in prior work as potentially having significant involvement in financial literacy, as well as staff of nonprofit organizations. A more extensive discussion of our scope and methodology appears in appendix I.

We conducted this performance audit from May 2011 to July 2012 in accordance with generally accepted government auditing standards. Those standards require that we plan and perform the audit to obtain sufficient, appropriate evidence to provide a reasonable basis for our findings and conclusions based on our audit objectives. We believe that the evidence obtained provides a reasonable basis for our findings and conclusions based on our audit objectives.

BACKGROUND

Financial literacy, which is sometimes also referred to as financial capability, has been defined as the ability to use knowledge and skills to manage financial resources effectively for a lifetime of well-being. Financial literacy encompasses financial education—the process whereby individuals improve their knowledge and understanding of financial products, services, and concepts. However, to make sound financial decisions, individuals need to be equipped not only with a basic level of financial knowledge, but also with the skills to apply that knowledge to financial decision making and behaviors.

The federal government plays a wide-ranging role in promoting financial literacy, and the multiagency Financial Literacy and Education Commission, which was created in 2003 by the Fair and Accurate Credit Transactions Act of 2003, was charged with, among other things, developing a national strategy to promote financial literacy and education, coordinating federal efforts, and identifying—and proposing means of eliminating—areas of overlap and duplication.[2] The commission is currently comprised of 21 federal entities; its Chair is the Secretary of the Treasury and its Vice Chair, as established in the Dodd-Frank Wall Street Reform and Consumer Protection Act (Dodd-Frank Act), is the Director of CFPB.[3] A wide variety of other organizations also provide financial literacy resources, including nonprofit community-based organizations; consumer advocacy organizations; financial services companies; trade associations; employers; and local, state, and federal government entities. Some financial literacy initiatives are aimed at the general population, while others target certain audiences, such as low-income individuals, military personnel, high school students, seniors, or homeowners.

Similarly, some financial literacy initiatives cover a broad array of concepts and financial topics, while others target specific topics, such as managing credit, investing, purchasing a home, saving for retirement, or avoiding fraudulent or abusive practices.

Efforts to improve financial literacy can take many forms. These can include one-on-one counseling; curricula taught in a classroom setting; workshops or information sessions; print materials, such as brochures and pamphlets; and mass media campaigns that can include advertisements in magazines and newspapers or on television, radio, or billboards. Many entities use the Internet to provide financial education, which can include information and training materials, practical tools such as budget worksheets and loan and retirement calculators, and interactive financial games. Youth-focused financial education programs are generally tied to a school curriculum.

FEDERAL AGENCIES SPENT ABOUT $68 MILLION ON FINANCIAL LITERACY ACTIVITIES IN FISCAL YEAR 2010

In fiscal year 2010, the federal government spent about $68 million on 15 of its 16 significant financial literacy programs and about $137 million on 4 programs providing housing counseling, which can include elements of financial education.

Costs for Financial Literacy Activities

We identified 16 significant financial literacy programs or activities within the federal government in fiscal year 2010.[4] As seen in table 1, the estimated cost for 15 of these programs and activities was $68 million.[5] This figure does not include estimated costs for CFPB, which was created during fiscal year 2010, or costs related to housing counseling, which is discussed separately.

Two of these federal financial literacy programs or activities were funded through a congressional appropriation for the specified program. The Excellence in Economic Education Program was appropriated about $1.45 million in fiscal year 2010, and the Department of Education obligated almost all of the amount to fund a single 5-year grant to a national nonprofit education organization. The National Education and Resource Center on Women and

Retirement Planning was appropriated $249,000 for fiscal year 2010, and the Department of Health and Human Services obligated about $246,000 of that amount that year.

Table 1. Estimates for Costs of 16 Federal Financial Literacy Activities, Fiscal Year 2010

Agency	Program or activity	FY 2010 estimate for portion of program costs attributed to financial literacy activities	Notes
Board of Governors of the Federal Reserve System	Division of Consumer and Community Affairs and Office of Public Affairs	$1,029,885	Estimate of calendar year 2010 costs provided by agency staff
Consumer Financial Protection Bureau	Office of Financial Education and other offices	Not applicable	Agency had not yet been created at the beginning of FY 2010
Department of Agriculture	Family and Consumer Economics programs	8,433,500	Estimate of FY 2010 costs provided by agency staff
Department of Defense	Personal Financial Management Program (located within Family Support Centers)	38,000,000	Estimate of FY 2010 costs provided by agency staff
Department of Education	Excellence in Economic Education Program	1,447,000	FY 2010 obligations
	Financial Education for College Access and Success Program	1,700,000	FY 2010 obligations
Department of Health and Human Services	National Education and Resource Center on Women and Retirement Planning	245,763	FY 2010 obligations

Table 1. (Continued)

Agency	Program or activity	FY 2010 estimate for portion of program costs attributed to financial literacy activities	Notes
Department of Labor	Saving Matters Retirement Savings Education Campaign	365,387	Estimate of FY 2010 costs provided by agency staff
	Wi$eUp	170,000	Estimate of FY 2010 costs provided by agency staff
Department of the Treasury	Office of Financial Education and Financial Access (including staff support for the Financial Literacy and Education Commission, and other initiatives)	1,300,000	Estimate of FY 2010 costs provided by agency staff
Federal Deposit Insurance Corporation	Money Smart Financial Education Program	2,749,594	Estimate of FY 2010 costs provided by agency staff
Federal Trade Commission	Division of Consumer and Business Education	784,904	Estimate of FY 2010 costs provided by agency staff
Office of the Comptroller of the Currency	Consumer education activities	450,000	Estimate of FY 2010 costs provided by agency staff.
Office of Personnel Management	Retirement Readiness NOW	200,000	Estimate of FY 2010 costs provided by agency staff

Agency	Program or activity	FY 2010 estimate for portion of program costs attributed to financial literacy activities	Notes
Securities and Exchange Commission	Office of Investor Education and Advocacy	2,000,000	Estimate of FY 2010 costs provided by agency staff
Social Security Administration	Financial Literacy Research Consortium	9,221,000	Estimate of FY 2010 costs provided by agency staff
Total		**$68,097,033**	

Source: GAO analysis based on federal budget documents and cost estimates provided by agency staff.

For most of the other programs, financial literacy activities were typically not organized as separate budget line items or cost centers within federal agencies. Instead, financial literacy activities were often one element of a broader effort that itself may or may not have had discrete funding. In these cases, we asked agency staff to estimate the portion of program costs that could be attributed to financial literacy activities. This typically entailed estimating the cost for the portion of staff time devoted to financial literacy, and sometimes also included the cost of contracts, printing, or other resources related to financial literacy activities. Because the methods for estimating costs varied, these costs may not be fully comparable across agencies.

We did not collect comprehensive information for costs subsequent to fiscal year 2010, but spending on many financial literacy programs has been in flux since that time. For example, the Social Security Administration's Financial Literacy Research Consortium and the Financial Education for College Access and Success Program did not receive new funding in fiscal years 2011 or 2012, and the Excellence in Economic Education Program did not receive funding for fiscal year 2012. In addition, at least two agencies—the Department of the Treasury (Treasury) and the Board of Governors of the Federal Reserve System— told us that their staffing resources devoted to financial literacy have declined since 2010. We did not identify any new federal financial literacy programs created since fiscal year 2010 other than CFPB, which was being formed as an agency that year.

Costs for Housing Counseling Activities

As shown in table 2, two federal agencies and a federally chartered nonprofit corporation spent about $136.6 million on housing counseling efforts during fiscal year 2010.[6] We have separated out the costs of housing counseling from other financial literacy activities because financial education typically is only a limited aspect of most housing counseling, which often largely consists of one-on-one assistance to address individual situations.

As seen above, the Department of Housing and Urban Development (HUD) obligated about $65.4 million during fiscal year 2010 for its Housing Counseling Assistance Program, which it used for certifying and overseeing housing counseling providers, training housing counselors, and providing counseling agencies with competitive grants. HUD also has 15 other active programs that have some housing counseling component or allow some portion of their funding to be used for housing counseling.[7] In addition, NeighborWorks America, a federally chartered nonprofit corporation, was appropriated $65 million for the National Foreclosure Mitigation Counseling Program during fiscal year 2010, of which it expended $59.4 million in grants for counseling, $3 million for training counselors, and $2.6 million for administrative purposes, according to agency staff. The organization also estimated that it spent about $2 million on other housing counseling activities—primarily prepurchase counseling—from funds it received through a separate congressional appropriation.[8] Treasury's Financial Education and Counseling Pilot Program, created by the Housing and Economic Recovery Act of 2008, provided $4.15 million in grants during fiscal year 2010 to provide counseling to prospective homebuyers.[9] Congress designated $3.15 million for an eligible organization in Hawaii, and Treasury also selected three additional organizations to receive grants.

In general, funding for housing counseling has varied in recent years. For example, HUD received no appropriated funds for its Housing Counseling Assistance Program in fiscal year 2011, but funding was restored to $45 million in fiscal year 2012. The agency has requested $55 million for the program in its fiscal year 2013 budget request, which it said would help support the Office of Housing Counseling, a new office created by the Dodd-Frank Act. The Financial Education and Counseling Pilot Program was appropriated no funds in fiscal years 2011 and 2012.

Some Federal Financial Literacy Efforts Overlap and May Offer Opportunities for Consolidation

Financial Literacy Efforts Are Spread across Multiple Federal Agencies

Federal financial literacy efforts are carried out by multiple federal programs and agencies. As shown in table 3, in fiscal year 2010 there were 16 significant federal financial literacy programs or activities among 14 federal agencies, as well as 4 housing counseling programs among 2 federal agencies and a federally chartered nonprofit corporation. These programs and activities covered a wide range of topics and target audiences and used a variety of delivery mechanisms.

Table 2. Estimates for Costs of Four Federal Housing Counseling Programs, Fiscal Year 2010

Agency	Program or activity	FY 2010 estimate	Notes
Department of Housing and Urban Development	Housing Counseling Assistance Program	$65,420,000	FY 2010 obligations
Department of the Treasury	Financial Education and Counseling Pilot Program	4,150,000	FY 2010 appropriation
NeighborWorks America	National Foreclosure Mitigation Counseling Program	65,000,000	FY 2010 obligations
	Other housing counseling activities	2,000,000	Estimate of FY 2010 costs provided by agency staff
Total		**$136,570,000**	

Source: GAO analysis based on federal budget documents and cost estimates provided by agency staff.

Table 3. Description and Target Audience for Significant Federal Financial Literacy and Housing Counseling Programs and Activities, Fiscal Year 2010

Financial Literacy			
Agency	**Program or activity**	**Description**	**Target audience**
Board of Governors of the Federal Reserve System	Division of Consumer and Community Affairs and Office of Public Affairs	Up-to-date web resources on regulatory changes regarding financial products and services, calculators, and information and tools on terms and disclosures for credit card accounts, overdraft protection programs, gift cards and credit scores. Website offers resources for teachers and students of various ages and knowledge levels via educational games, classroom lesson plans, online publications, and multimedia tools.	Adult consumers and students
Consumer Financial Protection Bureau	Office of Financial Education and other offices	The Office of Financial Education, Office of Service member Affairs, Office of Fair Lending and Equal Opportunity, and Office of Financial Protection for Older Americans plan to develop and implement initiatives to educate and empower consumers in general and specific target groups to make info-rmed financial decisions.	Consumers, service-members and their families, individuals who are 62 years or older
Department of Agriculture	Family and Consumer Economics programs	The National Institute of Food and Agriculture provides funding to land-grant colleges and universities and to state	Youth, rural families, elderly, other financially

Agency	Program or activity	Description	Target audience
		and county extension offices to support research and education, including outreach events related to personal financial topics.	vulnerable populations
Department of Defense	Personal Financial Management Program (located within Family Support Centers)	Personal financial managers on military installations provide financial education programs and counseling services designed to help servicemembers reach their financial goals. Services range from consultation on financial management, budgeting, and saving, to debt reduction strategies, consumer advocacy and complaint resolution, financial workshops, retirement planning, housing issues and referrals, and education programs for youth and teens.	Service-members and their families
Department of Education	Excellence in Economic Education Program	Competitive grant awarded to an organization that conducts activities, and makes subgrants to other organizations, to improve the quality of student understanding of personal finance and economics.	Students in kindergarten through grade 12
	Financial Education for College Access and Success Program	Supports state-led efforts to develop, implement, and evaluate personal finance instructional materials and teacher training intended to aid students in making financial aid decisions in relation to postsecondary education.	Students in middle and high-school—generally grades 6-12

Table 3. (Continued)

Agency	Program or activity	Description	Target audience
Department of Health and Human Services	National Education and Resource Center on Women and Retirement Planning	Provides women access to a one-stop gateway on retirement, care giving, health, and planning for long-term care.	Low-income women, women of color, women with limited English proficiency
Department of Labor	Saving Matters Retirement Savings Education Campaign	Workplace campaign to promote retirement savings and understanding of federal retirement law using interactive web tools, print publications, website, public service announcements, seminars, workshops, videos, and webcasts.	Employees, employers, small businesses
	Wi$eUp	Eight-module financial education curriculum targeting women that covers topics that include money basics, credit, saving and investing, insurance, retirement planning, and financial security. Offered online or in a classroom setting.	Generation X and Y women
Department of the Treasury	Office of Financial Education and Financial Access	A variety of financial literacy activities, including Money Math (four-lesson curriculum integrating personal finance and math topics), the National Financial Capability Challenge (provides teaching resources and encouragement and tests high school students on	All populations

Agency	Program or activity	Description	Target audience
		personal finance topics), Bank On USA (program encouraging access to mainstream financial institutions), MyMoney. gov (website on federal financial literacy resources), and staff support for the Financial Literacy and Education Commission.	
Federal Deposit Insurance Corporation	Money Smart Financial Education Program	Eleven-module financial education curriculum for adults designed to enhance basic financial skills and create positive banking relationships, available in nine languages. Eight-module version is available for young adults. The curriculum is available in instructor-led, computer-based instruction, and podcast (Mp3) formats.	Low- to moderate-income adults outside the financial mainstream and youth ages 12-20
Federal Trade Commission	Division of Consumer and Business Education	Multi-media resources covering topics such as credit, credit repair, debt collection, job hunting, job scams, managing mortgage payments, avoiding foreclosure rescue scams, and identity theft.	Consumers
Office of the Comptroller of the Currency	Consumer education activities	Websites, consumer advisories, public service announcements, community outreach, and print and radio advertisements aimed at educating consumers about banking and other financial issues.	Consumers

Table 3. (Continued)

Agency	Program or activity	Description	Target audience
Office of Personnel Management	Retirement Readiness NOW	Retirement education strategy designed to provide information that will help federal employees plan for retirement and calculate the investment needed to meet retirement goals.	Federal employees
Securities and Exchange Commission	Office of Investor Education and Advocacy	Provides information to help individual investors evaluate current and potential investments, make informed decisions, and avoid fraud.	Investors
Social Security Administration	Financial Literacy Research Consortium	Supported 2-year cooperative agreements with Boston College, RAND Corporation, and the University of Wisconsin to develop innovative materials and programs to help Americans plan for a secure retirement.	Adults preparing for retirement
Housing Counseling and Foreclosure Mitigation			
Department of Housing and Urban Development	Housing Counseling Assistance Program	Certifies and oversees housing counseling providers. Provides competitive grants to approved housing counseling agencies that provide prepurchase and postpurchase counseling, assistance to renters, homeless populations, and those seeking to resolve mortgage delinquency. Counseling may take place in person, over the phone, or via a self-study	Low-to moderate-income families

Agency	Program or activity	Description	Target audience
		computer module or workbook.	
Department of the Treasury	Financial Education and Counseling Pilot Program	Competitive grants to organizations to provide financial education and counseling to prospective homebuyers.	Prospective homebuyers
NeighborWorks America	National Foreclosure Mitigation Counseling Program	Competitive grants to housing counseling agencies to provide one-on-one counseling services for foreclosure prevention.	Homeowners at risk of foreclosure
	Other housing counseling activities	Expendable grants for which housing counseling is an eligible activity.	Current and prospective homeowners

Source: GAO analysis based on information from federal agencies and interviews with agency staff.

In prior work, we cited a 2009 report that had identified 56 federal financial literacy programs among 20 agencies.[10] That report, issued by the RAND Corporation, was based on a survey conducted by Treasury and the Department of Education that had asked federal agencies to self- identify their financial literacy efforts. However, our subsequent analysis of these 56 programs found a high degree of inconsistency in how different agencies defined financial literacy programs or efforts and whether they counted related efforts as one or multiple programs. We believe that our count of 16 significant federal financial literacy programs or activities and 4 housing counseling programs is based on a more consistent set of criteria.[11] (See app. II for a crosswalk between the 56 programs cited in a previous report and the 20 programs highlighted in this report.) We defined "significant" financial literacy programs or activities as those that were relatively comprehensive in scope or scale— that is, financial literacy was a key element rather than a minimal component or tangential goal. We did not include programs or activities that (1) provided financial information related to the administration of the program itself—such as information on applying for student financial aid or evaluating Medicare choices—rather than information aimed at increasing the beneficiaries' financial literacy and comprehension more generally; (2) were purely internal to the agency, such as information provided to agency employees on their employment and retirement benefits; or (3) represented individualized services or advice, such as assistance with tax preparation.[12] Apart from the programs cited in the tables above, some additional federal agencies address financial literacy on a smaller scale. For example, the website of the Federal Deposit Insurance Corporation (FDIC) includes such things as tips on banking and protecting your money, and information on foreclosure prevention, identity theft, and deposit insurance. In addition, the website of the Commodity Futures Trading Commission provides information on fraud awareness and prevention related to trading futures and options.

Fragmentation of financial literacy programs has evolved over a number of years, as a result both of statutory requirements and efforts undertaken at the initiative of federal agencies in addressing their missions.[13] Congress directed the creation of some programs and initiatives, examples of which include the following:

- The Office of Personnel Management's Retirement Readiness NOW program and the development of a retirement financial literacy strategy for federal employees were required by the Thrift Savings Plan Open Elections Act of 2004.[14]
- The Financial Education and Counseling Pilot Program was created by the Housing and Economic Recovery Act of 2008.[15]
- The Financial Education for College Access and Success Program was authorized under the Fund for the Improvement of Education Program under the Elementary and Secondary Education Act of 1965.[16]
- The National Foreclosure Mitigation Counseling Program was authorized through the Consolidated Appropriations Act, 2008, which sought to address the mortgage foreclosure crisis by providing homeowner counseling and strengthening the nation's counseling capacity.[17]
- CFPB was created by the Dodd-Frank Act, which specified the creation of the bureau's Office of Financial Education and its role in promoting financial literacy.[18]

Other financial literacy programs were initiated by agencies as part of their mission. For example, in line with the Securities and Exchange Commission's (SEC) mission as the primary overseer and regulator of the U.S. securities markets, the agency created the Office of Investor Education and

Advocacy, which gives investors information to evaluate current and potential investments, make informed decisions, and avoid fraudulent schemes. Similarly, the Federal Trade Commission's (FTC) financial literacy efforts have stemmed from its responsibilities for enforcing laws and regulations against unfair or deceptive acts or practices and protecting consumers in the marketplace.

Having multiple federal agencies involved in financial literacy efforts can have certain advantages. Some agencies have deep and long-standing expertise and experience addressing a specific issue area. For example, HUD has long been a repository for information on housing issues, SEC on investment issues, and the Department of Labor and Social Security Administration on retirement issues. Some agencies also have deep knowledge and ties to particular populations and may be the most efficient and natural conduit to providing them with information and services, as with the Department of Defense's (DOD) role in providing financial information and counseling to servicemembers and their families. In addition, providing information from multiple sources or in multiple formats can increase consumer access and the likelihood of educating more people. We have previously reported that different populations respond to different types of delivery mechanisms, such as one-on-one credit counseling, employer-provided retirement seminars, and classroom-based education.[19]

At the same time, fragmentation increases the risk of inefficiency and duplication of efforts. Our detailed review of financial literacy efforts across the federal government has uncovered no duplication—that is, cases where two or more agencies or programs were engaging in the same efforts and providing the same services to the same beneficiaries. In our analysis of the 20 significant financial literacy and housing counseling programs, we found that programs and efforts had differing focuses in terms of subject matter, target audience, or delivery method. This finding is largely consistent with prior reviews of the federal government's financial literacy efforts. In 2006, the Financial Literacy and Education Commission reported that it had studied federal financial literacy programs or resources and said it found minimal overlap and duplication among programs, noting that even when different agencies' programs sometimes appeared similar, closer inspection revealed important differences in things like the target audience, delivery platform, or specific content. In response to a recommendation we made that the commission engage an independent third party to assess these issues, two subsequent studies were conducted. The first study, contracted by Treasury to assess federal programs, reported little evidence of duplication of programs or resources based on comparisons of the intended program goals and targeted audiences of the assessed programs and major resources.[20] The second study resulted in the previously discussed 2009 report by the RAND Corporation, which sought to create a comprehensive catalog of existing federal financial literacy programs. It did not identify clear duplication, but it did note that multiple areas of overlap in subject matter and target audiences warranted more thorough investigation.

Our review did identify cases of overlap—that is, multiple agencies or programs with similar goals and activities. For example, as shown earlier, in fiscal year 2010 there were four discrete housing counseling programs or activities, which were administered by HUD, NeighborWorks America, and Treasury.[21] HUD's Housing Counseling Assistance Program funded a wide range of housing counseling, including prepurchase and postpurchase counseling and counseling related to foreclosure mitigation and prevention of predatory lending, as well as counseling services for renters and homeless populations.[22] Treasury's Financial Education and Counseling Pilot Program had goals similar to HUD's program, although it focused solely on prepurchase counseling and was intended, in part, to establish innovative program models for organizations to carry out effective counseling services. NeighborWorks also provided some prepurchase counseling and administered the foreclosure mitigation counseling program designed to help homeowners work with lenders to cure delinquencies. HUD and NeighborWorks meet regularly and closely coordinate activities to be complementary, according to HUD staff.

Similarly, five different financial literacy programs were directed at youth or young adults in fiscal year 2010. Three of these programs—Money Smart for Young Adults, Money Math, and the National Financial Capability Challenge—delivered information on similar topics, such as saving, budgeting, and borrowing, largely via instructor-led lesson plans. The Excellence in Economic Education Program and the Financial Education for College Access and Success Program both supported the development of personal finance instructional materials and teacher training on personal finance. In addition, FTC addresses youth financial literacy through an interactive website where youth can play games, design advertisements, and learn about activities related to target marketing, supply and demand, privacy protection, and bogus offers. The website of the Board of Governors of the Federal Reserve System also offers interactive games and classroom activities on its website for youth and young adults. Treasury staff told us that while all of these programs serve youth or young adults, there are significant variations among them in approach and in content. The staff noted, for example, that the goal of the National Financial Capability Challenge is to encourage the teaching of financial topics, rather than to provide content, and that the curricula of the Money Math and Money Smart for Young Adults programs differ substantially from each other.

Another example of overlap can be found in two federal financial literacy programs designed specifically for adult women. The Department of Labor's Wi$eUp program targeted Generation X and Y women—women generally born between the mid-1960s and the mid-1990s—and the Department of Health and Human Services' National Education and Resource Center on Women and Retirement Planning targeted traditionally hard-to-reach women, such as low-income women, women of color, and women with limited English proficiency. Both programs cover some of the same topic areas, such as retirement planning, investing, and money basics such as budgeting, saving, and banking. However, staff at the Department of Labor and the Department of Health and Human Services noted that the programs target different users, have different goals, and engage in different activities—for example, Wi$eUp is an online and classroom curriculum, while the National Resource Center uses peer counselors and offers information through model programs, workshops tailored to meet special needs, and print and web-based publications.

Creation of CFPB May Provide Opportunities for Consolidation

Additional overlap is evident with the activities of CFPB, which was created by the Dodd-Frank Act and became a standing organization in July 2011. The act established within CFPB an Office of Financial Education and charged it with developing and implementing initiatives intended to educate and empower consumers to make better informed financial decisions. Specifically, the office was directed to provide opportunities for consumers to access, among other things, financial counseling; information to assist consumers with understanding credit products, histories, and scores; information about savings and borrowing tools; and assistance in developing long-term savings strategies and wealth building. The duties of this office are in some ways similar to those of Treasury's Office of Financial Access, Financial Education, and Consumer Protection, a small office that also seeks to broadly improve Americans' financial literacy.[23] Treasury established this office in 2002 and tasked it with developing and implementing financial education policy initiatives and overseeing and coordinating Treasury's outreach efforts. Further, the Dodd-Frank Act charged CFPB with developing and implementing a strategy on improving the financial literacy of consumers, even though the Financial Literacy and Education Commission already has its own statutory mandate to develop, and update as necessary, a national strategy for financial literacy. CFPB staff told us that its own national strategy for financial literacy will serve as an operating plan that is distinct from, but broadly aligned with, the commission's national strategy. Staff involved in financial literacy from Treasury and CFPB told us that they meet regularly and that the two agencies are working closely together to ensure collaboration and avoid duplication.

CFPB also has other offices that are charged with financial literacy duties that are in some ways similar to those of other federal agencies. For example, the Dodd-Frank Act created within CFPB an Office of Servicemember Affairs, which is responsible for, among other things, developing and implementing initiatives intended to educate servicemembers and their families and empower them to make better informed decisions regarding consumer financial products and services, monitoring complaints, and coordinating efforts among federal and state agencies regarding consumer protection measures. These activities potentially overlap with those of DOD, whose Personal Financial Managers on military installations provide financial educational programs, partnerships, counseling, legal protections, and other resources designed to help servicemembers and their families. Staff of CFPB's Office of Servicemember Affairs told us that the office has been actively reaching out to servicemembers where they live in order to assess their needs, and between January 2011 and May 2012, the office held 84 events attended by more than 24,000 people and visited 37 military installations and National Guard units. Staff also told us that they have taken several steps to avoid duplicating DOD's Financial Readiness Program. For example, they said they will be focusing on reaching servicemembers in the Delayed Entry Program, a period prior to boot camp during which DOD does not yet engage in financial education. In addition, CFPB staff said they have been meeting monthly with DOD's Deputy Assistant Secretary of Defense for Military Community and Family Policy and his staff to coordinate their activities to avoid duplication across agencies. CFPB and DOD have also developed two Joint Statements of Principles, one on how they are going to handle complaints and the other on educational efforts and small-dollar lending.

In addition, CFPB and several other agencies provide financial literacy services that target older Americans. The Dodd-Frank Act created the Office of Financial Protection for Older Americans within CFPB and charged the office to develop goals for programs that provide financial literacy and counseling to help seniors recognize the warning signs of unfair, deceptive, or abusive practices, and protect themselves from such practices. These activities potentially overlap with those of FTC, which also plays a role in helping seniors avoid unfair and deceptive practices. For example, FTC has provided information to seniors on a range of topics, such as obtaining credit over the age of 62, avoiding charity fraud, recognizing and reporting telemarketing fraud, and avoiding scammers who may pose as friends, family, or government agencies. In an effort to work together and avoid duplication, CFPB and FTC finalized a memorandum of understanding in January 2012 to help, among other things, cooperate on consumer education efforts, promote consistency of messages, and maximize the use of educational resources. The Dodd- Frank Act also charged the Office of Financial Protection for Older Americans to develop goals for programs that provide one-on-one financial counseling on long-term savings and later-life economic security. As discussed earlier, the Department of Labor's Saving Matters Retirement Savings Education Campaign also plays a role in educating consumers on retirement issues and the Social Security Administration had a special initiative, as part of an earlier strategic plan, to encourage saving and to inform the public about its programs. In January 2012, staff at CFPB told us that the Office of Financial Protection for Older Americans had only recently become fully staffed and that the office had begun working with other federal and state agencies to identify best practices for educating and counseling senior citizens, identifying unfair and deceptive practices targeting this population, and advocating on their behalf.

Other potential areas of overlap include CFPB's Office of Fair Lending and Equal Opportunity, which plays a role in providing education on fair lending, as do the Office of the Comptroller of the Currency, FDIC, and FTC. CFPB has also created an Office for Students to work with complaints and questions regarding student loans. However, the Department of Education already has a number of web-based tools in place to help students understand financial aid and student loans. CFPB staff told us that one key distinction is that CFPB addresses private student loans, while the Department of Education addresses federally supported student loans. They also noted that they are coordinating with the Department of Education and have developed a memorandum of understanding with the department, and have jointly designed a standard student loan award letter and fact sheet.

The Dodd-Frank Act gave CFPB a primary role in addressing financial literacy, and the agency's Office of Financial Education—staffed at 10 full-time equivalents as of June 2012—has significant financial literacy resources relative to many other agencies. Yet there are similarities in mission between CFPB's statutory responsibilities and those of certain other federal entities. As we have noted in the past, federal programs contributing to the same or similar results should collaborate to help ensure that goals are consistent and, as appropriate, program efforts are mutually reinforcing.[24] Collaborating agencies should work together to define and agree on their respective roles and responsibilities and, in doing so, clarify who will do what and organize their joint and individual efforts. As noted above, during its initial development, CFPB has been meeting with other federal entities to coordinate their efforts. Ensuring clear delineation of the respective roles and responsibilities between CFPB and agencies with overlapping financial literacy responsibilities is essential to help ensure efficient use of resources.

The creation of multiple efforts within the federal government to address financial literacy has been the result of both legislation and initiatives within agencies. We have noted in the past that fragmentation in government programs often is the result of an adaptive and responsive federal government.[25] As new needs were identified, the common response has been a proliferation of responsibilities and roles to federal departments and agencies, perhaps targeted to a new audience or involving a new subject area. However, overlap and fragmentation among government programs or activities can, in some circumstances, lead to inefficiency, and the President and some members of Congress have set a goal of reorganizing and consolidating federal agencies to reduce the number of overlapping government programs.[26] In addition, as noted earlier, the multiagency Financial Literacy and Education Commission was charged by statute with proposing means of eliminating overlap and duplication among federal financial literacy activities.[27] The creation of CFPB, which will play a primary role in financial literacy, provides an opportunity for the commission and its member agencies to consider options for consolidating federal financial literacy efforts, which could help ensure the most efficient and effective use of federal resources in this area. While our February 2012 report stated that we expected to suggest that Congress consider options for such consolidation, the commission is better positioned to do so and this would be consistent with its statutory responsibility to address overlap and duplication.

Agencies Coordinate Their Efforts, but Opportunities Exist to Better Address the Appropriate Allocation of Resources

In addition to CFPB's efforts cited above, there has been a significant amount of coordination among other federal agencies with regard to their financial literacy efforts, as well as evidence of collaboration among federal agencies and state, local, nonprofit, and private entities. The Financial Literacy and Education Commission has played a key role in fostering this coordination and collaboration. However, its national strategy does not include a discussion of the appropriate allocation of federal resources.

Coordination and Collaboration Occur through a Variety of Means

Federal agencies involved in addressing financial literacy have a variety of mechanisms for coordinating their efforts, examples of which include the following:

- The Government Interagency Group is a working group of program-level staff from federal agencies that address financial literacy. The group meets three times a year to share ideas and best practices. The group is organized by the American Savings Education Council, a nonprofit organization and national coalition of public and private sector institutions focused on savings and retirement planning.
- The Department of Education, FDIC, and the National Credit Union Administration signed an agreement in November 2010 designed to encourage partnerships between schools, financial institutions, federal grantees, and other stakeholders to educate students about saving, budgeting and making wise financial decisions.
- SEC has partnered with the Department of Labor to develop guidance to help individuals understand the operations and risks of target-date fund investments, which are often mutual funds that change automatically to become more conservative as the fund's target date approaches. SEC has also worked with the Internal Revenue Service to include an insert about SEC's investor education resources,

including its Investor.gov education website, in the mailing of tax refund checks.

- As part of its Retirement Financial Literacy and Education Strategy for federal employees, the Office of Personnel Management has efforts under way to provide training and tools to the benefits officers of individual federal agencies, and to identify existing resources that federal agencies might use for the financial education of their employees.
- The Department of Labor and the Social Security Administration have worked together with AARP—a nonprofit organization focused on people age 50 and over—to host workshops for workers nearing retirement.

In addition to interagency coordination, the federal government has certain mechanisms in place to coordinate or partner with nonfederal entities, including states and localities and nonprofit and private entities. In January 2010, the President's Advisory Council on Financial Capability was created by executive order.[28] The council was tasked with a number of specific charges, including advising the President and the Secretary of the Treasury on: financial education efforts, promoting financial products and services that are beneficial to consumers (especially low- and moderate-income consumers), and promoting understanding of effective use of such products and services. In its January 2012 interim report, the council recommended that Treasury support a newly created private- sector award program recognizing employers that provide outstanding financial education to their employees.[29] The council meets regularly and has established subcommittees to address issues related to research and evaluation, partnerships between the public and private sectors, expanding financial access to low- and moderate-income households, and youth.

To facilitate and advance financial literacy at the state and local levels, the Financial Literacy and Education Commission created the National Financial Education Network for State and Local Governments in April 2007. Network members include state and local agencies and national organizations that share information through activities including periodic conference calls and a web-based database of financial literacy projects and programs.

Some federal agencies also partner with nonprofit and private organizations to expand outreach. Many federal agencies are members of Jump$tart Coalition for Personal Financial Literacy, a nonprofit partnership that focuses on financial literacy for young adults. Treasury partnered with

Jump$tart, the University of Missouri-St. Louis and Citigroup to develop Money Math: Lessons for Life, a financial literacy curriculum supplement for educators. FDIC has signed collaboration agreements or reached informal agreements with more than 1,200 active "alliance members" that promote or enhance the implementation of its Money Smart curriculum. Alliance members include financial institutions, schools or other educational service providers, military installations, community-based organizations, faith-based groups, employment and training service providers, government agencies, and other organizations. Likewise, the Board of Governors of the Federal Reserve System participates in Bank On USA programs, which are locally led coalitions of government agencies, financial institutions, and community organizations that focus on financial education and access for individuals and families who do not use mainstream financial institutions.

Federal agencies also collaborate with nonfederal entities with regard to financial literacy through the process of administering grants. For example, HUD provides training, guidance, and technical assistance to a network of community-based counseling agencies that it funds through its Housing Counseling Assistance Program. HUD also works with NeighborWorks, which is partially funded through HUD, in implementing the National Foreclosure Mitigation Counseling Program. Additionally, the Department of Agriculture collaborates with land-grant universities on financial literacy projects through grants provided by its National Institute of Food and Agriculture.[30] Also, DOD has collaborated with land-grant universities to offer programs and classes for military families and veterans.

Federal agencies have also collaborated with academic researchers and organizations on financial literacy research and product development. For example, in October 2008, Treasury and the Department of Agriculture convened a National Research Symposium on Financial Literacy and Education that sought to identify gaps in existing research and develop research priorities. Twenty-nine experts in the fields of behavioral and consumer economics, financial risk assessment, and financial education evaluation joined to summarize existing financial research findings, identify gaps in the literature, and define and prioritize questions for future analysis. In addition, through the Financial Literacy Research Consortium funded in fiscal years 2009 and 2010, the Social Security Administration worked with Boston College, RAND Corporation, and the University of Wisconsin to develop financial literacy educational tools and programs focusing on retirement savings and planning.

The Financial Literacy and Education Commission Has Improved Coordination but Has Not Addressed Resource Allocation

In general, we found that coordination and collaboration among federal agencies with regard to financial literacy has improved in recent years, in large part due to the efforts of the Financial Literacy and Education Commission. As noted earlier, the commission is currently comprised of 21 federal entities and was charged with, among other things, coordinating federal financial literacy efforts and promoting partnerships among federal, state, and local governments; nonprofit organizations; and private enterprises. Before the formation of the commission, agencies had no formal mechanism within the federal government through which to coordinate on financial literacy activities. In a 2006 report, we noted that the commission enhanced communication and collaboration among agencies involved in financial literacy by creating a single focal point for federal agencies to come together on the issue of financial literacy. The commission also developed a national strategy that included calls to action on interagency efforts.[31] Additional activities undertaken by the commission to foster coordination or collaboration include the following:

- *Meetings and working groups.* The commission holds formal meetings three times per year and, at the staff level, has several working groups, each represented by several federal agencies, including teams devoted to implementing the national strategy, promoting research and evaluation, and improving financial access.
- *MyMoney.gov website.* The commission was charged by statute with developing a financial education website that provides a coordinated point of entry for information about federal financial literacy programs and grants. The commission launched the MyMoney.gov website in October 2004.
- *Clearinghouse of research and resources.* The commission is in the process of developing a clearinghouse of federal research and resources on financial literacy. This clearinghouse will aggregate financial literacy research and information across federal agencies in one public website.
- *Reviews of federal activities.* As discussed earlier, the commission and Treasury contracted for two reports that cataloged and reviewed financial literacy efforts across the federal government, which helped

inform federal agencies of each other's activities and foster opportunities for coordination and collaboration.

In April 2006, the Financial Literacy and Education Commission issued a national strategy, which it was required by law to develop and modify as necessary, and in December 2010, it issued *Promoting Financial Success in the United States: National Strategy for Financial Literacy 2011.*[32] In our 2006 report, we found that the commission's first national strategy was a useful first step in focusing attention on financial literacy but was largely descriptive rather than strategic. We noted that the strategy only partially included certain characteristics that we consider to be desirable in any national strategy, including a description of resources required to implement the strategy. Our review of the 2011 national strategy indicates that it still does not fully address this element. An effective national strategy should include a discussion of resources, describing what a strategy will cost, the sources and types of resources needed, and where those resources should be targeted. The 2011 national strategy discusses the consumer education resources that the federal government makes available to consumers, and it sets building public awareness of these resources as a goal. However, the 2011 strategy still does not address the level and type of resources needed to implement the strategy, nor does it review the budgetary resources available to federal agencies for financial literacy efforts and how they might best be allocated. We have noted in the past that the governance structure of the commission presents challenges in addressing resource issues: it relies on the consensus of more than 20 federal agencies, has no independent budget, and has no legal authority to compel member agencies to take any action.[33] However, the commission does have the ability to at least identify resource needs and make recommendations or provide guidance on how Congress or federal agencies might allocate scarce federal financial literacy resources for maximum benefit. Without a clear description of resource needs, policymakers lack information to help direct the strategy's implementation, and without recommendations on resource allocations, policymakers lack information to help ensure the most efficient and effective use of federal funds. Additionally, addressing resource needs and allocations in the commission's national strategy would facilitate its statutory responsibility, discussed earlier, to propose means of eliminating overlap and duplication among federal financial literacy activities.

Overall Effectiveness of Federal Financial Literacy Programs Is Difficult to Measure, but Additional Evaluation Efforts Are Under Way

Most federal financial literacy activities include an evaluation component, but variation in the types of activities and the methods of evaluation create challenges in comparing results across programs. As we reported in June 2011, relatively few evidence-based evaluations of financial literacy programs have been conducted, limiting what is known about which specific methods and strategies—and which federal financial literacy activities—are most effective.[34] Several federal agencies have efforts under way seeking to determine the most effective approaches and programs.

Agencies Assess Their Financial Literacy Efforts in Various Ways

The wide range of federal financial literacy programs and activities and their evaluation metrics and methods, makes it difficult to systematically assess overall effectiveness or compare results across programs. Among the 20 significant federal financial literacy and housing counseling programs that we reviewed, we found that nearly all had assessed or measured their activities in some manner and, where feasible, many had undertaken some method of seeking to measure outcomes. Some of these evaluations sought to assess the effect of the program on the actual behavior of program participants and some assessed the effect of the program on knowledge, attitudes, or anticipated behavior. As we have reported in the past, in general the ultimate goal of financial education is to favorably affect consumer behavior, such as to promote improved saving and spending habits and wise use of credit. As such, financial literacy program evaluations are most reliable and effective when they measure the programs' impact on consumers' behavior. While there is fairly extensive literature on financial literacy in general, relatively few evaluations of financial literacy programs have been published that use empirical evidence to measure a program's impact on the participants' behavior.[35]

In addition, there are many significant challenges to rigorous and definitive evaluations of financial literacy programs. Outcome-based evaluation can be expensive and methodologically challenging, particularly long-term evaluation using a controlled experimental methodology, which can be especially time and labor intensive.[36] As well, measuring a change in participant behavior is much more difficult than measuring a gain in knowledge, which can often be captured through a simple exam at program completion. Some financial literacy programs and activities, such as those using broadcast media to disseminate information, may also simply not be well-suited to outcome-based evaluation because the program has no direct contact with the intended audience. Further, given the many variables that can affect consumer behavior and decision making, ascribing long-term changes to a particular program is difficult. In addition, some program activities, such as posting a webpage, may be too small in scope to warrant conducting an outcome evaluation study, so tracking output measures—such as the number of individuals served or the volume of materials distributed—may be the only feasible option. One academic review of financial literacy evaluations found that the majority of financial literacy programs it reviewed measured only program outputs.[37]

Among the federal financial literacy programs and activities we reviewed, we identified a number of cases in which evaluation included at least some assessment of the effect on consumer behavior of activities operated or funded by federal agencies:

- *National Foreclosure Mitigation Counseling Program.* NeighborWorks contracted with the Urban Institute for a study resulting in a series of reports, the most recent of which was published in December 2011, which evaluated program outcomes of the federally funded National Foreclosure Mitigation Counseling program. The study found that among homeowners who received loan modifications, those who received counseling under the program were more likely to avoid entering foreclosure, successfully cure existing foreclosures, or obtain favorable loan modifications than those who did not receive the counseling.[38]
- *U.S. Army personal financial management training.* In 2009, staff at the Board of Governors of the Federal Reserve System conducted a study of a U.S. Army personal financial management training, which included a 2-day financial education course taught by college staff for young servicemembers enlisted at a Texas army base. Participants were surveyed on their financial behaviors 6 months after completing the course and compared with a control group of soldiers who did not take the course. After controlling for other factors, the study found

that the financial education course did not have a significant effect on most of the soldiers' financial behaviors, such as comparison shopping, saving, and paying bills on time.[39]

- *Money Smart.* FDIC collaborated in an independent evaluation of the Money Smart program in 2003 that measured its effectiveness on a sample of adult program participants who did not have accounts at banks or other mainstream financial institutions. The study found that 80 percent of those who completed Money Smart said they intended to open a bank account, although it did not collect data on whether they actually did so.[40] A second study conducted by FDIC in 2007 surveyed individuals prior and subsequent to their participation in the program and also followed up by telephone 6 to 12 months after their final class. It found that participants were more likely to open deposit accounts, save money in a mainstream deposit product, use and adhere to a budget, and experience greater confidence in their financial abilities.[41] However, this study did not have the benefit of a control group—that is, it did not measure participants in the program against a comparison group that did not participate in the program. FDIC is currently evaluating the effect of Money Smart for Young Adults on the financial knowledge and behavior of young adults (ages 12 to 20). The agency said it expects the evaluation to be completed by the end of 2013.
- *HUD housing counseling*. In 2008, HUD published a report that presented a systematic overview of the housing counseling industry and HUD-approved housing counseling providers.[42] In May 2012, two reports were published resulting from the Housing Counseling Outcome Evaluation. The first report looked at a sample of individuals who received foreclosure mitigation counseling from HUD-funded and HUD-approved agencies between August 2009 and December 2009.[43] The findings indicated that 18 months after initiating foreclosure counseling, 56 percent of homeowners were in the home and current on their payments, 28 percent were in the home and behind on their payments, and 16 percent were out of the home. However, the study did not include a control group to compare this group of homeowners to others who had not received foreclosure counseling. The second report examined prepurchase counseling and found that 35 percent of the study participants had become homeowners 18 months after seeking prepurchase counseling; this study also did not include a control group.[44] HUD is in the process of

conducting an additional prepurchase counseling demonstration and impact evaluation that will track up to 6,000 individuals to examine the effectiveness of different housing counseling delivery methods compared to a control group of individuals not receiving counseling. Data collection is expected to begin around September 2012, and an initial report is expected by May 2014.

- *Financial Literacy Research Consortium.* In 2009 the Social Security Administration established a Financial Literacy Research Consortium that funded 63 research projects at three academic centers on a range of consumer financial behavior and retirement savings issues. According to agency staff, 11 of these projects included evaluations of the effectiveness of interventions designed to improve consumer financial literacy. For example, one study funded through the consortium at the University of Wisconsin found that a 5-hour online financial education module led to modest increases in knowledge of financial issues, but no changes in self-reported financial behaviors 3 months later.[45] Another project has randomly assigned 600 homebuyers to varying combinations of financial planning interventions to be completed during the first year after home purchase.[46] The project is ongoing, and evaluation of the effectiveness of the interventions will be conducted in subsequent years.[47]
- *U.S. Department of Agriculture Family and Consumer Economics programs.* The Department of Agriculture encourages land-grant institutions receiving grants for financial literacy activities to conduct some form of evaluation, and some grantees have sought to evaluate program outcomes. For example, researchers at Ohio State University examined the outcomes of a youth curriculum designed to enhance money management skills. Three months after the completion of the program, more than 80 percent of students in 6th-12th grades reported improvements in the extent to which they repaid money on time, set aside money for the future, and compared prices.[48]
- *Financial Education for College Access and Success Program.* In 2010, the U.S. Department of Education's Financial Education for College Access and Success Program provided a grant to the Tennessee Department of Education to measure the program's effect on student knowledge, attitudes, and behaviors, including rates of financial aid form completion, college enrollment, decisions regarding financial aid, and use of financial products and services. Agency officials said that the study will also measure the effect of the project

on the knowledge, attitudes, and instructional skills of participating teachers. Results of the study were not available as of May 2012.

- *Financial Education and Counseling Pilot Program.* Treasury requires the homebuyer counseling organizations that receive program grants to periodically report on the results of two output goals (numbers served and hours of service provided) and three outcome goals chosen by the grantees (such as changes in participant savings, credit scores, or debt). As of April 2012, limited information was available about the program's impact because grantees had provided outcome data no earlier than 2011, while some of the desired outcomes of their programs can take years to realize.[49]
- *Wi$eUp.* As of 2010, more than 19,000 individuals had participated in Wi$eUp's eight-module financial education curriculum. The program tracks the percentage of participants who, as a result of their participation, reduced their debt and increased their savings or investments. Individuals complete pre- and postassessments for each module and are asked to complete a 3-month follow-up assessment to determine the financial changes they have made. Sixty-nine percent of participants in programs conducted in 2009 by Texas A&M's AgriLife Extension reported reducing their debt by a median of $500 since taking the Wi$eUp course, and 62 percent reported increasing their savings or investments.

Some agencies that we reviewed, while not assessing program effect on participant behavior, have reported on the effect on participant knowledge or attitudes or have future plans for evaluating behavior:

- *Excellence in Economic Education Program.* In 2009, program subgrantees gave standardized tests to 6,040 middle and high school students and 894 teachers shortly after they had completed the economics and personal finance instructional activities of the Excellence in Economic Education Program. Fifty-eight percent of students participating in projects funded through the program scored proficient on standardized tests of economics, personal finance, or both, compared to their target goal of 70 percent. In addition, 82 percent of teachers participating in the projects showed a significant increase in their scores on a standardized measure of economic content knowledge, as compared to the target goal of 70 percent.

- *Federal Reserve System.* Staff of the Board of Governors of the Federal Reserve System told us that the board does not conduct assessments of its financial literacy activities. However, some regional Federal Reserve Banks—which are part of the system but are not themselves federal agencies—do assess their own financial literacy activities. For example, the Federal Reserve Bank of Atlanta, in partnership with the Federal Reserve Bank of St. Louis, used third-party experts to conduct a 2-year assessment of the effectiveness of their financial literacy programs and materials, as well as to design and test tools for measuring knowledge gains and behavior changes.
- *DOD Family Support Centers.* DOD is in the second phase of the Military Family Life Project, a longitudinal department-wide survey of 40,000 married active-duty servicemembers and 100,000 military spouses designed to capture the long-term impact of deployment on families and to improve the support provided to them. According to DOD staff, one purpose of the study is to assess the financial readiness of servicemembers. In addition, DOD staff told us that as part of a larger evaluation effort of its family support programs, DOD is collaborating with a team of researchers from Pennsylvania State University to develop outcome measures for the department's financial readiness campaign and the services of its personal finance counselors. While the outcomes to be measured are still being determined, they may include changes in servicemembers' financial knowledge and behaviors, the staff said.
- *Consumer Financial Protection Bureau.* CFPB's financial literacy efforts have not been in place long enough for evaluation, but staff told us that evaluation will be a key component of its financial literacy activities and, as discussed later in this report, the bureau's Office of Financial Education contracted with a third party with specialized expertise to help assess the effectiveness of financial literacy programs.

Outcome-based evaluation is not always well suited for some financial literacy efforts, such as those that use mass media or distribute informational materials broadly. As such, several federal financial literacy programs that we reviewed collect information largely on output measures, such as number of individuals served or the volume of materials distributed. In some instances, the programs also measure the degree to which customers are satisfied with the service provided.

- *Federal Trade Commission.* FTC's Division of Consumer and Business Education tracks its financial literacy activities based on materials distributed and webpages accessed by consumers and businesses. It reported that in 2010 it distributed more than 17 million publications and its consumer and business education websites were accessed more than 26 million times.
- *Office of the Comptroller of the Currency.* The agency collects data on the number of website hits, media placements, audience reach, and the dollar value of donated air time for its public service announcements. In fiscal year 2011, it ran four media campaigns related to financial literacy, which included print and radio features in English and Spanish that appeared 14,079 times in 44 states. Its Consumer Education websites received 699,904 visits.
- *SEC Office of Investor Education and Advocacy.* SEC measures the number of investors its education efforts reach, which was 17.8 million in fiscal year 2010. SEC staff told us they are planning a future evaluation that will include, among other things, customer satisfaction with usefulness of investor education programs and materials. In addition, the Dodd-Frank Act directed SEC to submit by July 21, 2012, a study of retail investors' financial literacy, which must identify "the most effective existing private and public efforts to educate investors."
- *National Education and Resource Center on Women and Retirement Planning.* Staff at the Department of Health and Human Services told us they had not evaluated the program, but that the nonprofit administering the program had distributed more than 3,000 copies of publications and training materials available at conferences and workshops directed to the financial services industry, women's groups, advocacy groups, and senior centers.
- *Treasury's Office of Financial Access, Financial Education, and Consumer Protection.* The office collects participation statistics for its National Financial Capability Challenge, which provides teaching resources and encouragement and tests high school students on personal finance topics, and reported 84,372 students and 2,517 educators participating in 2011. The program also collects and publicly reports on average scores (by state and nationally), perfect scores, and students in the top 20 percent of scores nationally and by state.

- *Saving Matters Retirement Savings Education Campaign.* The Department of Labor conducts surveys at the program's seminars and webcasts as part of an in-house evaluation process. The evaluations, conducted with the assistance of the Gallup Organization, assess the number of participants reached by the program, usefulness of the program, and satisfaction of participants, with a goal of an 85 percent satisfaction rate on its seminars, workshops, and webcasts. The department also tracks attendance at these events, the distribution of its publications, and the use of interactive online tools, videos, and webcast archives.

Several Efforts to Better Assess Effectiveness Are Under Way

As discussed previously, several federal financial literacy programs—such as Money Smart for Young Adults, HUD's Housing Counseling Assistance Program, and the DOD Financial Readiness Campaign—are in the early stages of significant evaluations that may provide information about program effectiveness in the future. In addition to those evaluations of individual agency efforts, certain other federal efforts are under way that apply across agencies and seek more broadly to understand the most effective methods and strategies for improving financial literacy.[50]

- *Financial Literacy and Education Commission.* The 2011 national strategy and its implementation plan set as one of its four goals identifying, enhancing, and sharing effective practices. As previously discussed, Treasury staff told us that the commission has begun to establish a clearinghouse of evidence-based research and evaluation studies, current financial topics and trends of interest to consumers, innovative approaches, and best practices. According to Treasury staff, the clearinghouse will be available through the MyMoney.gov website and will have links to research and data sets from federally supported financial literacy projects. The clearinghouse is being developed by a contractor but will be maintained by Treasury and is expected to be available around September 2012. In addition, the commission's Research and Evaluation Working Group is charged with encouraging multidisciplinary research and sharing effective practices among federal agencies. In May 2012, the working group released a report on research questions and priorities that is intended to inform federal agencies, researchers, and others on the most important questions facing the field of financial literacy and to help make best use of limited research dollars.[51]

- *CFPB's Office of Financial Education.* CFPB's Office of Financial Education recently contracted with The Urban Institute for a financial education program evaluation project, which seeks to increase understanding of which interventions can improve financial decision-making skills in consumers. The effectiveness of selected financial education programs will be evaluated using a data collection tool and will be tested against a control group. Staff told us they intend to use the insights from the study to provide direction to practitioners about how to design and support effective financial capability and money confidence programs. A report is expected to be issued in the spring of 2014. In addition, CFPB's Office of Financial Education has collaborated with its Office of Research to develop metrics for financial education, according to agency staff.
- *Office of Personnel Management.* As part of its Retirement Readiness NOW program, the Office of Personnel Management is developing a rating system to determine which federal agencies are most effective in providing financial literacy and retirement education to the civilian labor force. According to agency staff, the ranking system is intended to help hold federal agencies accountable for their retirement education plans and strategies.
- *Treasury's Office of Financial Access, Financial Education, and Consumer Protection.* This office has contracted out a research project assessing financial capability outcomes for both youth and adults, with results expected by the end of 2012. The office will test the hypothesis that increased financial capability—including financial information and education and access to simple, low-cost, transaction and savings products—will enhance the financial stability and well-being of low- and moderate-income individuals and households.

CONCLUSION

Federal financial literacy and housing counseling resources are spread across many federal agencies, the result of both legislation and programs evolving to address a variety of populations or topics. While we uncovered no duplication, some agencies or programs do have overlapping goals and activities, which raises the risk of inefficiency and underscores the importance of coordination. The creation of CFPB adds a new player to the mix. The agency will play a primary federal role in addressing financial literacy, yet some of its responsibilities overlap with those of other federal agencies. Effective collaboration among agencies entails defining and agreeing on respective roles and responsibilities and organizing collective efforts. CFPB appears to be making progress thus far in coordinating with federal agencies that have overlapping financial literacy responsibilities, but ensuring clear delineation of respective roles and responsibilities will also be essential to ensure efficiency. Moreover, the creation of CFPB may signal an opportunity for reconsidering how the federal government's financial literacy efforts are organized. In particular, some consolidation of these efforts could help ensure the most efficient and effective use of federal financial literacy resources. While our February 2012 report stated that we expected to suggest that Congress consider options for such consolidation, the Financial Literacy and Education Commission is better positioned to identify possible options and this would be consistent with the commission's statutory responsibility to propose means of eliminating overlap and duplication among federal financial literacy activities.

Overall, coordination among federal agencies with regard to financial literacy has improved in recent years, and the commission has played a critical role in this. The commission's 2011 national strategy includes some elements that may be useful in guiding federal financial literacy efforts, but it could do more to identify the resources needed to implement the strategy and how federal resources might best be allocated among programs and agencies, characteristics we have found to be desirable for any national strategy. The commission faces the constraints of lacking its own budget or legal authority over member agencies to take any action, but, even so, it has the ability to provide recommendations or guidance to Congress or federal agencies. Without a clear discussion of resource needs and where resources should be targeted, policymakers lack information to help direct the strategy's implementation and help ensure efficient use of funds.

We found that nearly all significant federal financial literacy programs that we reviewed had assessed or measured their activities in some manner and many had undertaken some method of seeking to measure outcomes. While some measured the effect on participant behavior, often they assessed changes in participant knowledge or tracked output measures, such as the number of consumers reached. There is only limited knowledge about which federal financial literacy programs are most effective in achieving the key goal of improving consumer behavior, in large part because of the cost and difficulty of measuring these outcomes. Rigorous outcome-based evaluation is not necessarily practical or appropriate for every program, but its promotion and use, where feasible, is important to help Congress and federal agencies focus financial literacy resources on the most effective approaches and activities. In our February 2012 report, we stated that we expected to recommend that Congress consider requiring federal agencies to evaluate the effectiveness of their financial literacy efforts. However, we have found that the new initiatives that CFPB, Treasury, and the Financial Literacy and Education Commission have under way to assess effectiveness and identify best practices are positive steps in this direction. As a result, based on these ongoing efforts, we no longer believe that this recommendation is necessary at this time.

RECOMMENDATIONS FOR EXECUTIVE ACTION

We recommend that as part of its ongoing coordination efforts, the Consumer Financial Protection Bureau take steps to help ensure clear delineation of the respective roles and responsibilities between itself and other federal agencies that have overlapping financial literacy responsibilities.

To help ensure effective and efficient use of federal financial literacy resources, we also recommend that the Secretary of the Treasury and the Director of the Consumer Financial Protection Bureau, in their capacity as Chair and Vice Chair of the Financial Literacy and Education Commission, and in concert with other agency representatives of the commission:

- identify for federal agencies and Congress options for consolidating federal financial literacy efforts into the activities and agencies that are best suited or most effective, and
- revise the commission's national strategy to incorporate clear recommendations on the allocation of federal financial literacy resources across programs and agencies.

AGENCY COMMENTS AND OUR EVALUATION

We provided a draft of this report to the Departments of Agriculture, Defense, Education, Health and Human Services, Housing and Urban

Development, Labor, and the Treasury, as well as to the Board of Governors of the Federal Reserve System, Consumer Financial Protection Bureau, Federal Deposit Insurance Corporation, Federal Trade Commission, Office of the Comptroller of the Currency, Office of Personnel Management, Securities and Exchange Commission, and the Social Security Administration. We incorporated technical comments provided by these agencies as appropriate. In addition, CFPB, the Department of Health and Human Services, and Treasury provided written responses.

In its response, CFPB neither agreed nor disagreed with the recommendations addressed to it, but it highlighted steps that its Offices of Financial Education, Servicemember Affairs, and Financial Protection for Older Americans are taking to delineate roles and responsibilities, improve coordination, and avoid duplication with other federal agencies. CFPB also noted that it is committed to ensuring that its activities are informed by data and analytics. For example, it cited a project it has launched that uses rigorous quantitative methodologies to assess the effectiveness of several existing financial education programs and provide direction to practitioners about how to design and support effective programs on improving consumers' financial capability and confidence about money.

Treasury said that it agreed with our recommendations to the Financial Literacy and Education Commission related to identifying options for consolidation and making recommendations on the allocation of federal financial literacy resources. Treasury noted that the department has already begun work with other members of the commission to define specific and measurable objectives that will help agencies assess the impact of their financial capability activities, which will provide a framework for any resource allocation recommendations the commission may have.

The Department of Health and Human Services said in its response that it disagreed that its National Education and Resource Center on Women and Retirement Planning overlapped with the Department of Labor's Wi$eUp program because the two programs have differing methodologies, approaches, and target populations. We acknowledge the differences between the two programs in our report. However, the definition for overlap presented in this report is "multiple agencies or programs with similar goals and activities," and we believe that this accurately applies to these two programs, both of which are financial literacy programs designed for adult women.

Alicia Puente Cackley
Director, Financial Markets and Community Investment

APPENDIX I. OBJECTIVES, SCOPE, AND METHODOLOGY

Our objectives were to address (1) what is known about the cost of federal financial literacy activities; (2) the extent and consequences of overlap and fragmentation among financial literacy activities; (3) what the federal government is doing to coordinate its financial literacy activities; and (4) what is known about the effectiveness of federal financial literacy activities. For the purposes of our analysis, we considered duplication to occur when two or more agencies or programs are engaged in the same activities and provide the same services to the same beneficiaries. Overlap refers to when multiple agencies or programs have similar goals, engage in similar activities or strategies to achieve them, or target similar users. Fragmentation refers to circumstances in which more than one federal agency is involved in the same broad area of national need. Our report focuses largely on federal programs or activities that were relatively comprehensive in scope or scale and included financial literacy as a key component rather than a tangential goal. We generally excluded from our review programs or activities for which financial literacy was only a minimal component; that provided financial information related to the administration of the program itself rather than information aimed at increasing the beneficiaries' financial literacy and comprehension more generally; that were purely internal to the agency; or that provided individualized financial services or advice rather than education. Using these criteria, we identified 16 significant financial literacy programs and 4 significant housing counseling programs in operation in fiscal year 2010.

To address our first objective, we collected and reviewed the President's Budget for fiscal years 2010, 2012, and 2013; budget justifications, as needed; congressional appropriations; and other sources that included cost information. For many federal agencies, financial literacy activities were not organized as separate budget line items or cost centers. In these cases, we asked agency staff to estimate the portion of program costs that could be attributed to financial literacy activities for fiscal year 2010, which is the year for which we reported costs. This typically entailed estimating the cost of that portion of staff time devoted to financial literacy, as well as the cost of contracts, printing, or other resources related to financial literacy activities. Because the methods for estimating costs varied, these costs may not be fully comparable across agencies. To assess the reliability of these estimates, we interviewed agency staff about their cost estimation methodology, what their estimate included, and what assumptions they used in making the estimate. Although costs may not be comparable across the agencies because agencies used differing methodologies, we determined that the data are reliable for the purposes of generally estimating federal dollars spent on financial literacy activities.

To address our second and third objectives, we reviewed a 2009 report by the RAND Corporation that cataloged federal financial literacy efforts; reports from the President's Advisory Council on Financial Capability; the national strategies and supporting documents of the Financial Literacy and Education Commission; and other reports as appropriate. We also reviewed the commission's MyMoney.gov website and the websites of individual federal agencies related to financial literacy. In addition, we reviewed federal agency strategic plans; performance and accountability reports; budget justifications; memorandums of understanding between agencies or with nonfederal entities; and laws related to financial literacy activities or programs. Further, to assess the extent of overlap or duplication, we collected and analyzed characteristics of federal financial literacy programs and identified similarities and differences among programs' purposes, subject matter content, targeted populations, and delivery methods. We assessed the commission's 2011 National Strategy for Financial Literacy, in part, by benchmarking it against our prior work that identified the general characteristics of an effective national strategy.[52] Those recommended characteristics for national strategies had been developed by reviewing several sources of information, which included the Government Performance and Results Act of 1993; legislative and executive branch guidance for national strategies; general literature on strategic planning and performance; and our prior work on issues related to planning, integration, implementation, and other related subjects.

To determine what is known about the effectiveness of federal financial literacy activities, we collected evaluations, as well as any available information on the outputs or outcomes of these activities. As applicable, we reviewed output data such as information on numbers of program participants or consumers reached, website visits, and copies of publications or other materials distributed that were available through a variety of sources. For example, as available, we reviewed results of surveys of customer satisfaction, attitudes, or intention to change behavior, and tests that measured changes in program participants' knowledge. In addition, we reviewed information on program effect that appeared in agencies' strategic plans and performance and accountability reports. We also reviewed the 2009 RAND report, which included self- reported information from federal agencies on methods they have used to evaluate their financial literacy programs, and we updated this information as necessary through interviews with agency staff. In addition, we collected any available studies and evaluations that had been conducted on the outcomes of federal financial literacy activities, which included evaluations conducted by the agencies themselves or by external researchers. Each of the studies and evaluations cited in our report was reviewed for methodological reliability and determined to be sufficiently reliable for our purposes.

Finally, to address all four of our objectives, we interviewed staff who address financial literacy issues at 17 federal agencies that we had identified in prior work as potentially having significant involvement in financial literacy—the Board of Governors of the Federal Reserve System; Consumer Financial Protection Bureau; Departments of Agriculture, Defense, Education, Health and Human Services, Housing and Urban Development, Labor, and Treasury; Federal Deposit Insurance Corporation; Federal Trade Commission; Internal Revenue Service; Office of the Comptroller of the Currency; Office of Personnel Management; Securities and Exchange Commission; Social Security Administration; and the U.S. Mint. We also interviewed staff at NeighborWorks America (a federally chartered nonprofit corporation) and representatives of the National Financial Education Network of State and Local Governments, the President's Advisory Council on Financial Capability, and two nonprofit organizations, the American Savings Education Council and the National Endowment for Financial Education.

We conducted this performance audit from May 2011 to July 2012 in accordance with generally accepted government auditing standards. Those standards require that we plan and perform the audit to obtain sufficient, appropriate evidence to provide a reasonable basis for our findings and conclusions based on our audit objectives. We believe that the evidence obtained provides a reasonable basis for our findings and conclusions based on our audit objectives.

APPENDIX II. CROSSWALK BETWEEN FEDERAL FINANCIAL LITERACY PROGRAMS IDENTIFIED IN THE RAND REPORT AND PROGRAMS SELECTED FOR INCLUSION IN THIS REPORT

In 2009, the Departments of the Treasury and Education asked federal agencies to self-identify their financial literacy efforts, which resulted in a 2009 report by the RAND Corporation that identified 56 federal financial literacy programs among 20 agencies.[53]

Agency	Programs identified in 2009 RAND report		Programs and activities cited in this report (GAO-12-588)
Consumer Financial Protection Bureau			1. Office of Financial Education and other offices
Commodity Futures Trading Commission	1. www.cftc.gov	●	
Department of Agriculture	2. Financial Security Program		2. Family and Consumer Economics programs
Department of Defense	3. Financial Readiness Campaign		3. Personal Financial Management Program (located within Family Support Centers)
Department of Education	4. Cooperative Civic Education and Economic Exchange Program	●	
	5. Excellence in Economic Education Program		4. Excellence in Economic Education Program
			5. Financial Education for College Access and Success Program
Department of Health and Human Services	6. Own Your Future Long-Term Care Awareness Campaign	●	
	7. National Education and Resource Center on Women and Retirement Planning		6. National Education and Resource Center on Women and Retirement Planning
	8. Pension Counseling and Information Program	▲	
	9. Aging and Disability Resource Center	●★	
	10. Medicare Improvements for Patients and Providers Act	●★	
	11. Medicaid Program Eligibility	●★	
	12. Medicare Options Compare	●★	
	13. Medicare Prescription Drug Plan Finder	●★	
	14. Insure Kids Now Hotline and Website	●★	
	15. Questions and Answers about Health Insurance: A Consumer Guide	●	
	16. Executive Leadership Development Program	●	
	17. Public Health Officer Basic Course	■	
	18. Pre-Retirement Seminar	■	

Reasons that program or activity does not fall within the scope of this engagement:

- ● Financial literacy was a minimal component
- ★ Related to administration of program
- ■ Employee benefits--internal to agency
- ✖ Discontinued after 2009
- ▲ Individualized services or advice

Agency	Programs identified in 2009 RAND report		Programs and activities cited in this report (GAO-12-588)
Department of Housing and Urban Development	19. Housing Counseling		7. Housing Counseling Assistance Program
Department of Labor	20. Saving Matters Retirement Savings Education Campaign		8. Savings Matters Retirement Savings Education Campaign
	21. WI$eUp		9. WI$eUp
	22. Health Benefits Education Campaign	●	
Department of the Treasury	23. National Financial Capability Challenge		10. Office of Financial Education and Financial Access
	24. Money Math: Lessons for Life		(10. Office of Financial Education and Financial Access)
	25. Financial Education and Counseling Pilot Program		11. Financial Education and Counseling Pilot Program
	26. Community Financial Access Pilot	✖	
Department of Veterans Affairs	27. Financial Literacy Education Program	■	
Federal Deposit Insurance Corporation	28. Money Smart Financial Education Program		12. Money Smart Financial Education Program
	29. FDIC Consumer Protection Resources	●	
	30. FDIC Deposit Insurance Coverage Resources	●★	
Federal Reserve Board	31. Financial education initiatives		13. Division of Consumer and Community Affairs and Office of Public Affairs
Federal Trade Commission	32. Ftc.gov/moneymatters		14. Division of Consumer and Business Education
	33. Ftc.gov/freereports		(14.)
	34. Ftc.gov/youarehere		(14.)
	35. Ftc.gov/gettingcredit		(14.)
	36. Youtube.com/ftcvideos		(14.)
	37. Ftc.gov/idtheft		(14.)
	38. Ftc.gov/bizopps		(14.)
	39. Ftc.gov/hurricanerecovery		(14.)
U.S. Mint	40. Mint Education Initiative	●	
National Credit Union Association	41. Deposit Insurance Education Campaign	●★	

Reasons that program or activity does not fall within the scope of this engagement:

- ● Financial literacy was a minimal component
- ★ Related to administration of program
- ■ Employee benefits--internal to agency
- ✖ Discontinued after 2009
- ▲ Individualized services or advice

Figure 1. (Continued).

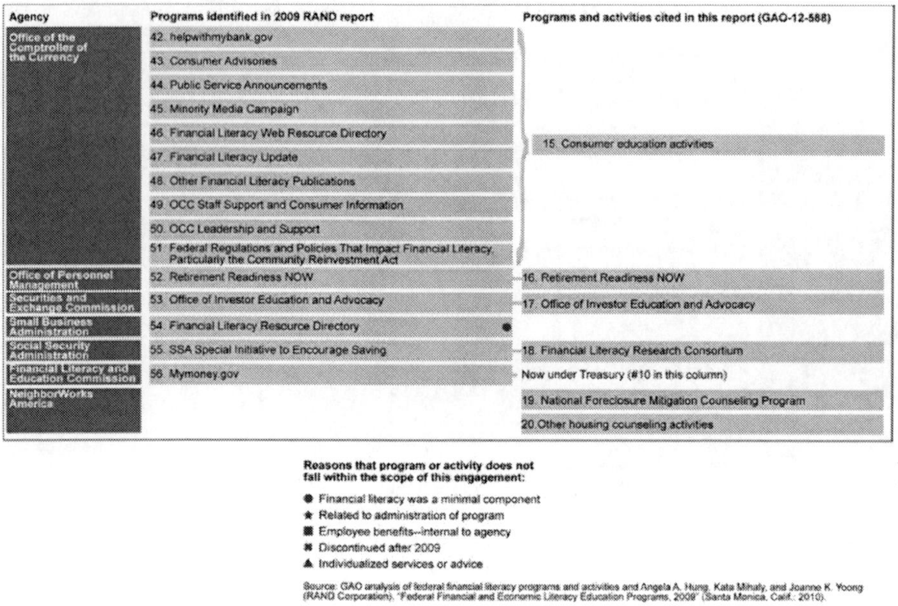

Figure 1. Crosswalk between Federal Financial Literacy Programs Identified in the RAND Report and Programs Selected for Inclusion in This Report (GAO-12-588).

We reported these results in a 2011 report, but our subsequent analysis of these 56 programs found a high degree of inconsistency in how different agencies defined financial literacy programs or efforts and whether they counted related efforts as one or multiple programs.[54] For the purposes of our current report, we developed criteria for identifying significant federal financial literacy and housing counseling activities and programs. We defined such activities or programs as those that were relatively comprehensive in scope or scale and for which financial literacy or housing counseling was a key objective rather than a tangential goal. As appropriate, we defined a related set of activities (such as a series of webpages from one agency) as a single program. In addition, we excluded programs or activities (1) for which financial literacy was only a minimal component; (2) that provided financial information related to the administration of the program itself rather that information aimed at increasing the beneficiaries' financial literacy and comprehension more generally; (3) that were purely internal to the agency, such as information provided to agency employees on their employment and retirement benefits; and (4) that represented individualized services or advice. We included as federal programs those of NeighborWorks America, a government-chartered, nonprofit corporation that receives federal funding for housing counseling, including through an annual appropriation from Congress. Finally, the RAND report was based on programs and activities in place in 2009, while our list reflects programs and activities in place during fiscal year 2010.

End Notes

[1] Public Law 111-139 required us to identify and report annually on federal programs, agencies, offices, and initiatives, either within departments or governmentwide, which have duplicative goals or activities. Pub. L. No. 111-139, § 21, 124 Stat. 29 (2010), 31 U.S.C. § 712 Note. For recent GAO work on potential duplication, overlap, and fragmentation among federal financial literacy programs, see GAO, *2012 Annual Report: Opportunities to Reduce Duplication, Overlap and Fragmentation, Achieve Savings, and Enhance Revenue*, GAO-12-342SP (Washington, D.C.: Feb. 28, 2012), pp. 151-154; *Follow-up on 2011 Report: Status of Actions Taken to Reduce Duplication, Overlap, and Fragmentation, Save Tax Dollars, and Enhance Revenue*, GAO-12-453SP (Washington, D.C.: Feb. 28, 2012), pp. 53-54; and *Opportunities to Reduce Potential Duplication in Government Programs, Save Tax Dollars, and Enhance Revenue*, GAO-11-318SP (Washington, D.C.: Mar. 1, 2011).

[2] Pub. L. No. 108-159, Title V, 117 Stat. 1952, 2003 (2003) (codified at 20 U.S.C. §§ 9701-08).

[3] Pub. L. No. 111-203, Title X, § 1013(d), 124 Stat. 1971, 1956 (2010), 20 U.S.C. § 9702(d).

[4] The program and cost data included in this report reflect fiscal year 2010 because these data were originally collected as part of our most recent effort to report on duplication, fragmentation, and overlap in federal programs (GAO-12-342SP), which used fiscal year 2010 as its time frame. We have defined "significant" as those financial literacy and education programs or activities that were relatively comprehensive in scope or scale and included financial literacy as a key objective rather than a tangential goal. Additional information about our criteria for significant programs or activities appears later in this report.

[5] This report updates cost information provided in our February 2012 report, GAO-12-342SP, which did not include cost information for the Office of Personnel Management and the Department of Defense. All costs are for fiscal year 2010, with the exception of the Board of Governors of the Federal Reserve System, costs for which are from calendar year 2010.

[6] Programs within other agencies, such as the Department of Defense and the Department of Veterans Affairs, also provide some elements of housing counseling.

[7] These programs are the Federal Housing Administration's Home Equity Conversion Mortgage; Community Development Block Grant; HOME Investment Partnerships Program; Second Mortgage Assistance for First-Time Homebuyers; Rural Housing Stability Grant Program; Public Housing Operating Fund; Section 8 Tenant-Based Rental Assistance Homeownership Option; Demolition and Disposition of Public Housing; Family Self-Sufficiency; Public Housing Resident Homeownership Programs; Conversion of Distressed Public Housing to Tenant-Based Assistance; Low Income Housing Preservation and Resident Homeownership Act Prepayment Options; Native American Housing Assistance and Self Determination Act Housing Block Grants; Native Hawaiian Housing Block Grants; and Section 8 Rental Assistance.

[8] According to NeighborWorks staff, in addition to its direct appropriations from Congress, NeighborWorks also received two grants from HUD related to housing counseling in fiscal year 2010. We have included the funding for those grants in the cost estimate for HUD rather than NeighborWorks. One grant was for $1,250,501 for comprehensive counseling,

and the second was for $500,000 for counseling under the Home Equity Conversion Mortgage program, which allows homeowners age 62 or older to tap into the equity in their homes by borrowing against the value of their home.

[9] Pub. L. No. 110-289, § 1132, 122 Stat. 2654, 2727 (2008) (codified at 12 U.S.C. §1701x Note).

[10] GAO, *List of Selected Federal Programs That Have Similar or Overlapping Objectives, Provide Similar Services, or Are Fragmented Across Government Missions*, GAO-11-474R (Washington, D. C.: Mar. 18, 2011); and GAO-11-318SP. Angela A. Hung, Kata Mihaly, and Joanne K. Yoong (RAND Corporation), "Federal Financial and Economic Literacy Education Programs, 2009" (Santa Monica, Calif.: 2010). http://www.rand.org/content/dam/rand/pubs/technical_reports/2010/RAND_TR857.pdf.

[11] Our review was based on programs in place in fiscal year 2010; as noted earlier, at least three of the programs in place at that time were not funded in fiscal year 2012.

[12] Although the financial literacy activities of the Department of Defense's Family Support Centers are largely internal to the agency, we made an exception and included them because they serve more than 7 million individuals and provide a broad range of counseling and services.

[13] We define fragmentation to refer to those circumstances in which more than one federal agency (or more than one organization within an agency) is involved in the same broad area of national need.

[14] Pub. L. 108-469, § 2, 118 Stat. 3892 (2004), 5 U.S.C. § 8350 Note.

[15] Pub. L. No. 110-289, § 1132, 122 Stat. 2654, 2727 (2008), 12 U.S.C. § 1701x Note.

[16] Elementary and Secondary Education Act of 1965, as amended, Pub. L. No. 89-10, 79 Stat. 27, 20 U.S.C. §§ 7243-7243b.

[17] Pub. L No. 110-161, Div. K, Title III, 121 Stat. 1844, 2441 (2008).

[18] Dodd-Frank Act, § 1011, 124 Stat. 1376, 1964 (2010), 12 U.S.C. § 5491.

[19] GAO, *Financial Literacy: A Federal Certification Process for Providers Would Pose Challenges*, GAO-11-614 (Washington, D.C.: June 28, 2011).

[20] Sarah Baughman, *Financial Literacy and Education Commission Independent Evaluation Final Report* (Blacksburg, Va.: May 25, 2009).

[21] Programs at DOD and the Department of Veterans Affairs also provide some elements of housing counseling. DOD's Military OneSource and Military and Family Life Consultant Program provide foreclosure counseling for servicemembers returning home from active duty abroad, and the Department of Veterans Affairs has loan counselors that address housing issues in its Regional Loan Centers to help veterans facing foreclosure or other financial problems.

[22] Prepurchase counseling generally helps potential homebuyers learn about buying a home and explains the financial responsibilities of homeownership. Postpurchase counseling includes topics such as foreclosure mitigation, budgeting, and home maintenance.

[23] In April 2012, Treasury changed the name of the Office of Financial Education and Financial Access to the Office of Financial Access, Financial Education, and Consumer Protection, and the office has taken on new functions related to consumer protection.

[24] GAO, *Results-Oriented Government: Practices That Can Help Enhance and Sustain Collaboration among Federal Agencies*, GAO-06-15 (Washington, D.C.: Oct. 21, 2005).

[25] GAO, *Managing for Results: Using the Results Act to Address Mission Fragmentation and Program Overlap*, GAO/AIMD-97-146 (Washington, D.C.: Aug. 29, 1997).

[26] For example, see Executive Office of the President, *Building a 21st Century Government by Cutting Duplication, Fragmentation, and Waste* (Washington, D.C.: Feb. 28, 2012).

[27] Pub. L. No. 108-159, § 514(f)(2)(d), 117 Stat. 1952, 2006 (Dec. 4, 2003) (codified at 20 U.S.C. § 9703(f)(2)(d)).

[28] Exec. Order No. 13,530, 75 Fed. Reg. 5481 (Jan. 29, 2010). Prior to the President's Advisory Council on Financial Capability, created by President Obama, there was the President's Advisory Council on Financial Literacy, which was created by executive order by President Bush in January 2008. Exec. Order No. 13,455, 73 Fed. Reg. 4445 (Jan. 22, 2008).

[29] U.S. Department of the Treasury, *Interim Report: President's Advisory Council on Financial Capability* (Washington D.C.: Jan. 18, 2012).

[30] A land-grant college or university is an institution of higher education designated by its state to receive certain federal benefits where the focus is to be on the teaching of agriculture, science, and engineering.

[31] GAO, *Financial Literacy and Education Commission: Further Progress Needed to Ensure an Effective National Strategy*, GAO-07-100 (Washington, D.C.: Dec. 4, 2006).

[32] Pub. L. No. 108-159, § 514(h), 117 Stat. 1952, 2004 (Dec. 4, 2003) (codified at 20 U.S.C. § 9703(h)). Financial Literacy and Education Commission, *Taking Ownership of the Future: The National Strategy for Financial Literacy* (Washington, D.C.: April 2006), and Financial Literacy and Education Commission, *Promoting Financial Success in the United States: National Strategy for Financial Literacy 2011* (Washington, D.C.: December 2010).

[33] GAO, *Financial Literacy and Education Commission: Progress Made in Fostering Partnerships, but National Strategy Remains Largely Descriptive Rather Than Strategic,* GAO-09-638T (Washington, D.C.: Apr.29, 2009).

[34] GAO, *Financial Literacy: A Federal Certification Process for Providers Would Pose Challenges,* GAO-11-614 (Washington, D.C.: June 28, 2011).

[35] GAO-11-614.

[36] A controlled experimental methodology is a research design that randomly assigns participants to treatment and control groups in order to rigorously analyze the effects of the studied activity.

[37] Angela C. Lyons, Lance Palmer, Koralalage S. U. Jayaratne, and Erik Scherpf, "Are We Making the Grade? A National Overview of Financial Education and Program Evaluation," *The Journal of Consumer Affairs* 40 (2006): 208-35.

[38] The Urban Institute, *National Foreclosure Mitigation Counseling Program Evaluation: Final Report, Rounds 1 and 2* (Washington, D.C.: December 2011).

[39] When controlling for multiple factors, the study found that the course did not have an impact on most financial behaviors, with the exception that soldiers who took the course were more likely than the comparison group to report using informal spending plans and less likely to report using formal spending plans. The authors controlled for the following additional factors: years in the military, pay grade, gender, education, race/ethnicity, marital status, premilitary experiences, and possession of a credit card. Catherine Bell, Daniel Gorin, and Jeanne M. Hogarth, *Does Financial Education Affect Soldiers' Financial Behavior?* (Terre Haute, Ind.: Networks Financial Institute, August 2009).

[40] Angela Lyons and Erik Scherpf, *An Evaluation of the FDIC's Financial Literacy Program Money Smart* (University of Illinois at Urbana-Champaign, May 2003).

[41] Federal Deposit Insurance Corporation, *A Longitudinal Evaluation of the Intermediate- term Impact of the Money Smart Financial Education Curriculum upon Consumers' Behavior and Confidence* (Washington, D.C.: Apr. 2007).

[42] Christopher E. Herbert, Jennifer Turnham, and Christopher N. Rodger, *The State of the Housing Counseling Industry*, Abt Associates Inc. for the U.S. Department of Housing and Urban Development (Cambridge, Mass.: Sept. 2008).

[43] Anna Jefferson, Jonathan Spader, Jennifer Turnham, and Shawn Moulton, *Foreclosure Counseling Outcome Study: Final Report*, Abt Associates Inc. for the U.S. Department of Housing and Urban Development (Cambridge, Mass.: May 2012).

[44] Jennifer Turnham, and Anna Jefferson, *Pre-Purchase Counseling Outcome Study: Research Brief,* Abt Associates Inc. for the U.S. Department of Housing and Urban Development (Bethesda, Md.: May 2012).

[45] J. Michael Collins, *Online Financial Education for Employees: A Randomized Experiment* (University of Wisconsin, CFS Research Brief (*FLRC 11-13*): October 2011).

[46] Stephanie Moulton, Cäzilia Loibl, J. Michael Collins, and Anya Savikhin, *Field Experiments on the Impacts of Financial Planning Interventions for Recent Homebuyers*, University of Wisconsin Center for Financial Security Working Paper, October 2011.

[47] Although the Financial Literacy Consortium received no new funding after fiscal year 2010, the Social Security Administration allowed three grantees funded by the consortium to use grant funds until September 29, 2012, to complete their projects.

[48] Lisa Sotak, Theresa M. Ferrari, Nancy W. Hudson, Graham Cochran, and Beth L. Bridgeman, *Outcomes of Participation in Real Money, Real World, 2007 Statewide Evaluation Final Report* , Ohio State University Extension, Mar. 17, 2008.

[49] For additional information on the program, see GAO, *Financial Education and Counseling Program,* GAO-11-737R (Washington, D.C.: July 27, 2011).

[50] In GAO-12-342SP, we stated that we expected to recommend that Congress consider requiring federal agencies to evaluate the effectiveness of their financial literacy efforts. Based on our subsequent review of the measures described in this section, we believe that such a recommendation is not necessary at this time.

[51] Financial Literacy and Education Commission, *2012 Research Priorities and Research Questions: Financial Literacy and Education Commission Research & Evaluation Working Group* (Washington, D.C.: May 2012).

[52] GAO-04-408T and GAO-07-100.

[53] Angela A. Hung, Kata Mihaly, and Joanne K. Yoong (RAND Corporation), "Federal Financial and Economic Literacy Education Programs, 2009" (Santa Monica, Calif.: 2010). http://www.rand.org/content/dam/rand/pubs/technical_reports/2010/RAND_TR857.pdf.

[54] GAO-11-318SP.

INDEX

R

S